WARSHIPS
WWII TO THE PRESENT DAY

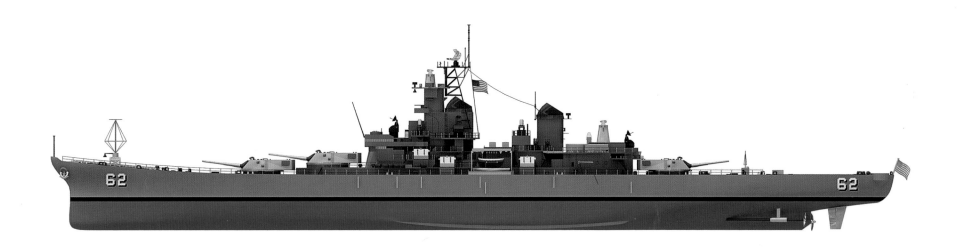

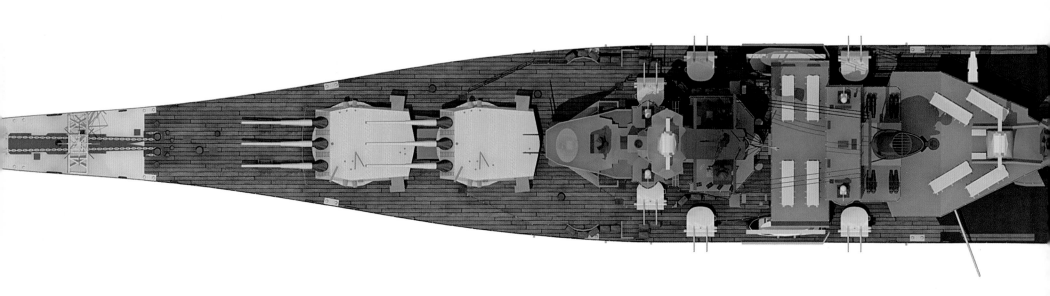

WARSHIPS
WWII TO THE PRESENT DAY

FEATURES SEVEN VIEWS OF EACH VESSEL

MARTIN J. DOUGHERTY

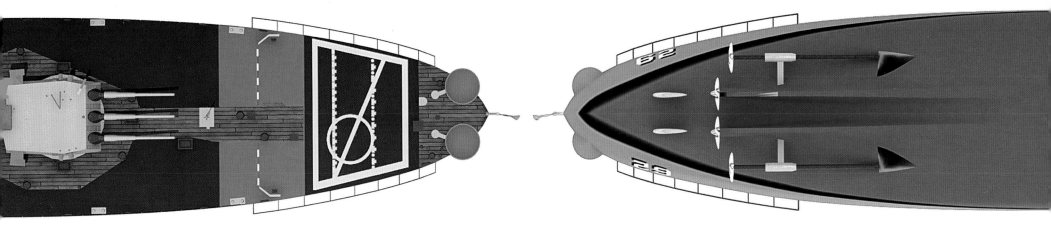

amber
BOOKS

This edition first published in 2011

Reprinted in 2011

Published by
Amber Books Ltd
Bradley's Close
74–77 White Lion Street
London N1 9PF
United Kingdom
www.amberbooks.co.uk

ISBN: 978-1-907446-54-2
Printed in China

Project Editor: James Bennett
Designer: Joe Conneally
Picture Research: Terry Forshaw

Digital illustrations courtesy of Military Visualizations, Inc.

Contents

Introduction

A naval vessel is more than a fighting platform. It is a symbol of national prestige and a political tool. It can carry out non-military missions such as disaster relief and the rescue of distressed vessels. The existence of a powerful navy can avert a war or encourage a diplomatic solution to a conflict. However, the purpose of warships is to fight if necessary, and to this end they need mobility, firepower and the ability to survive at least long enough to engage the enemy.

Increased Specialization

Until relatively recently, all warships could engage all targets. In the Age of Sail, the only opponents faced by a wooden sailing ship were cannon-armed warships and armed merchants, or shore batteries equipped with similar weapons. Specialist ammunition and techniques were available, but for the most part the choice of armament was a simple one – the biggest and most guns a ship could carry. Defence was a matter of stout timbers, good sailing qualities to deny the enemy a crippling shot, and powerful enough armament to win the fight before too much damage was taken.

However, modern technology has greatly complicated this equation. The advent of the submarine and the aircraft have

BISMARCK

PT–109

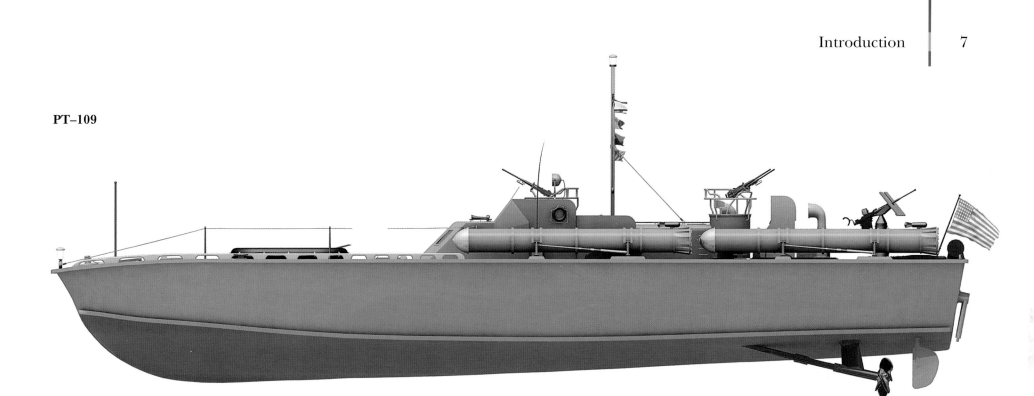

increased the range of possible threats considerably, while the invention of guided missiles, torpedoes and mines have made necessary whole new forms of defence.

Defence and Attack

A warship can be attacked in four broad ways: Gunfire, torpedoes, mines and airborne weapons. The latter category includes bombs and rockets delivered by helicopters and aircraft as well as missiles launched from the shore, other ships, aircraft or submarines. For the purposes of defence it does not matter much how the weapon is delivered; a torpedo will always attack from underwater no matter whether it is fired from a small boat, a submarine, or dropped from a helicopter, and a missile will always come in above sea level.

Conversely, the nature of the target is critical to the choice of weapon when on the offensive. Guns and missiles are of little use against a submarine while torpedoes cannot be fired at aircraft or land targets. Thus a warship must carry weapons suitable for the targets it expects to engage, and defences tailored to the weapons that are likely to attack it rather than the platforms they are launched from. In addition to weapons and defences, a warship needs a number of other critical systems. A propulsion system and sufficient fuel to allow a reasonable operating radius are of course necessary. Engines and propulsion systems are bulky, and subject to diminishing returns in terms of increased size versus vessel speed. An extremely fast vessel is expensive and must give up space to machinery that could be used for other systems. It will also get through fuel at a high rate, reducing range or requiring yet more internal space to be given over to mobility rather than fighting power.

Sensors and control systems are also vital. Radar guidance is important for weapon accuracy, while sonar is essential to give warning of a submarine in the vicinity. Without radar and other sensors, a vessel can only engage targets within visual range and even then the chances of a hit are low. The loss of a critical sensor system can 'mission kill' a warship, forcing it to abandon its mission and return to base for repairs even though its weapons and engines are intact.

Support Systems

In order to find targets, move and fight, a warship requires many other support systems. The crew need to eat and sleep, and suitable stations to do their work. They must be able to communicate within the vessel and to deliver reports and receive orders, to deal with casualties and damage to the ship, and crew the vessel with sufficient ease and comfort that they do not become excessively fatigued.

Many factors can contribute to the effectiveness or otherwise of a warship. Something as apparently trivial as awkward supply-handing systems can delay a replenishment operation and make the vessel unavailable for combat operations at a critical time.

SNOWBERRY

SEA SHADOW

A sensor system that is excellent when in top condition but which is prone to damage may represent a critical liability in combat. A tight design that crams immense capability into the hull at the expense of crew comfort may result in inefficiency during a long deployment as the personnel become fatigued and frustrated.

It has wisely been said that the groundwork for victory at sea is laid in procurement and design meetings, when the systems to go into a ship are decided upon and their layout is determined. Further advantage is accrued – or lost – from doctrine and tactics. The support of other vessels and the procedures used in combat can cover a ship's weaknesses and exploit its strengths, and vice versa. Finally, the morale and training of the crew and officers can make a huge difference to the effectiveness of the vessel. A single bad decision, or a moment of brilliance, can doom an otherwise excellent vessel or enable a poor one to beat the odds.

The creation of an effective warship requires balancing all the relevant factors; armament, defence, sensors, mobility, crew and support systems. It is not always obvious what the 'right' answer to this equation should be, especially when the additional constraints of cost and the ability to upgrade the vessel throughout its lifetime are considered. There is no guarantee that the vessel may have to fulfil an entirely different role than the one it was designed for; a lot can change during the lifetime of a naval vessel.

Some of the warships in the following pages are specialist designs built around a single role or mission concept. Some are mulitrole vessels designed to meet a range of challenges whether operating alone or while escorting other ships. Although many of these warships were designed to meet the same mission requirements, no two are exactly alike. Differences in technology and design philosophy have in some cases produced very different vessels capable of doing the same job.

Creating the Digital Models

Every ship in this book was originally created as a complex 3D object using computer graphics software commonly employed in the production of movies and video games. From the 3D model, each of the seven-view images was generated, or rendered, from various viewpoints (above, below, etc) around the model. The result is a set of highly detailed 2D images suitable for printing.

1 All 3D objects start with a single point, called a vertex. Its position in the virtual 'space' in the graphics program can be defined by three parameters: X, Y and Z or, in more basic terms, left and right, up and down and back and forth.

2 Once you have three vertices, they can be joined to form a 2D triangle in 3D space, called an edged face.

3 To begin creating a gun, for example, the computer graphics program 'lathes' hundreds of 2D shapes in the Z axis, drawing a barrel shape in three dimensions around the X axis. Every point is defined by different values for X and Y.

4 The end result is a 3D gun barrel. Although it appears solid, it is composed of hundreds of edged faces, themselves made up of lines and vertices.

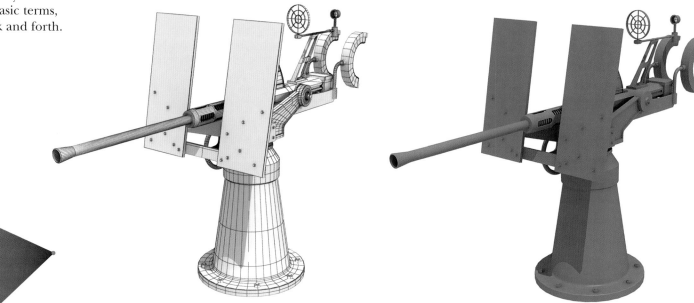

5 To create more complex objects, simple elements are fitted together to form an assembly like this complete Bofors anti-aircraft gun from USS *Yorktown*.

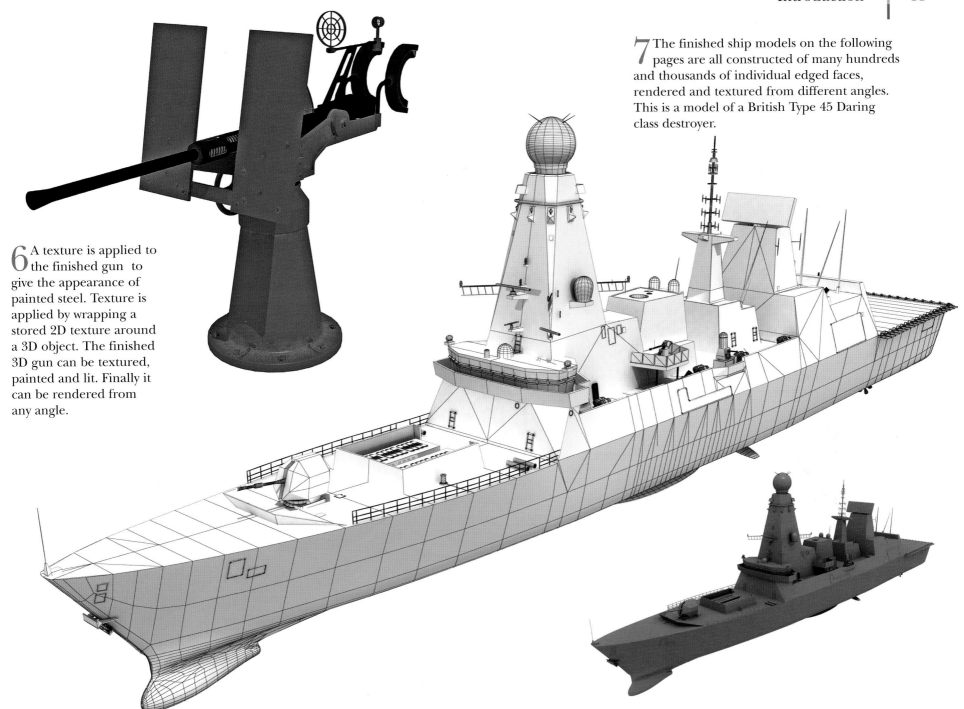

6 A texture is applied to the finished gun to give the appearance of painted steel. Texture is applied by wrapping a stored 2D texture around a 3D object. The finished 3D gun can be textured, painted and lit. Finally it can be rendered from any angle.

7 The finished ship models on the following pages are all constructed of many hundreds and thousands of individual edged faces, rendered and textured from different angles. This is a model of a British Type 45 Daring class destroyer.

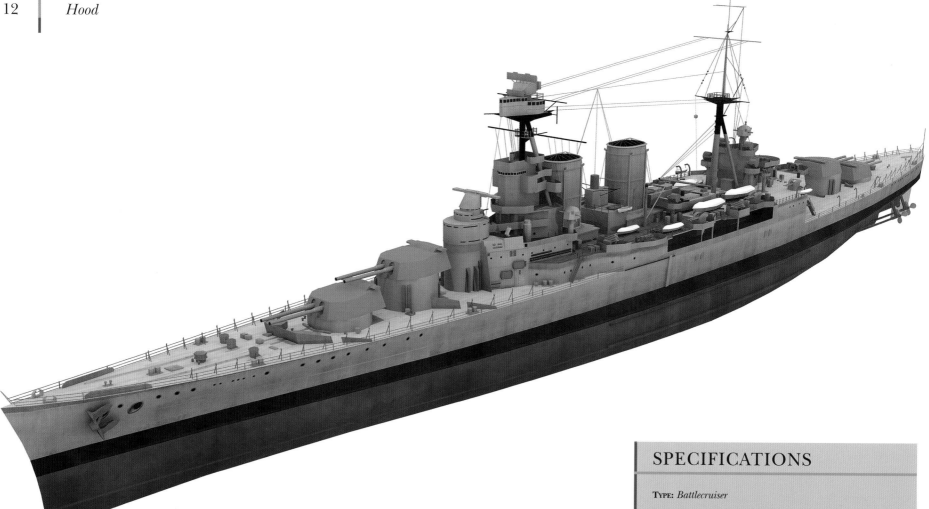

Hood

HMS *Hood* was the last battlecruiser commissioned into the Royal Navy. She was to have been lead ship of a class of four, but disenchantment with the battlecruiser concept resulted in cancellation of the follow-on vessels. At her commissioning in 1920, she was the world's largest warship. Although she was very lightly protected by capital ship standards, HMS *Hood* is often considered to be the first of the fast battleships, rather than a true battlecruiser. Her main armament when built comprised eight 381mm (15in) guns in twin turrets, plus twelve 140mm (5½in) guns and an extensive anti-aircraft battery, which was later upgraded. She also carried torpedo tubes and was refitted with anti-submarine 'unrotated projectile' launchers.

SPECIFICATIONS

TYPE: *Battlecruiser*

COUNTRY OF ORIGIN: *United Kingdom*

DISPLACEMENT: *47,430 tonnes (46,681 long tons)*

DIMENSIONS: *Length: 262.3m (861ft) Beam: 31.8m (104ft) Draught: 9.8m (32ft)*

MACHINERY: *4 x Brown-Curtis geared steam turbines, 4 shafts*

MAXIMUM SPEED: *28 knots (52km/h)*

ARMAMENT: *8 x 381mm (15in) BL Mk I guns; 14 x QF 101mm (4in) Mk XVI AA guns; 24 x QF 40mm (1.575in) 2-pounder 'pom pom' AA guns (1941)*

LAUNCHED: *1920*

Light Armour

HMS Hood *was redesigned during her construction to incorporate lessons learned at the Battle of Jutland. Even so, she remained lightly armoured compared to other capital ships and even the battlecruisers of some other nations. An extensive refit was scheduled for 1939, but was cancelled due to the outbreak of war. As a result* Hood *received only modifications to her lighter armament during her career.*

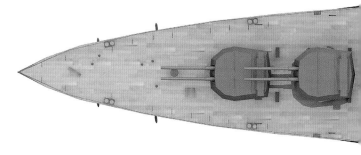

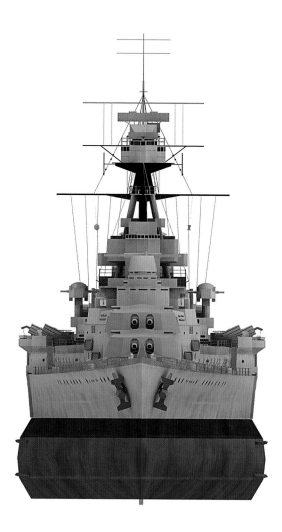

MAIN FEATURES

- Fast, well armed but lightly armoured capital ship
- Main battery equivalent to a battleship
- Largest warship in the world when commissioned

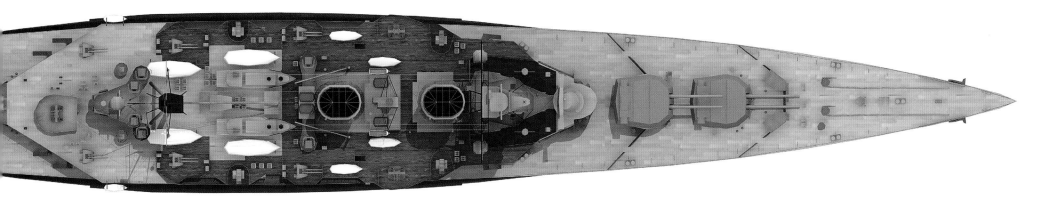

JEWEL IN THE CROWN

HMS Hood *was the pride of the Royal Navy for many years and spent much of her career on 'flag-showing' tours, which inevitably took their toll on her machinery. She was sunk in action against the* Bismarck *and* Prinz Eugen *in 1940.*

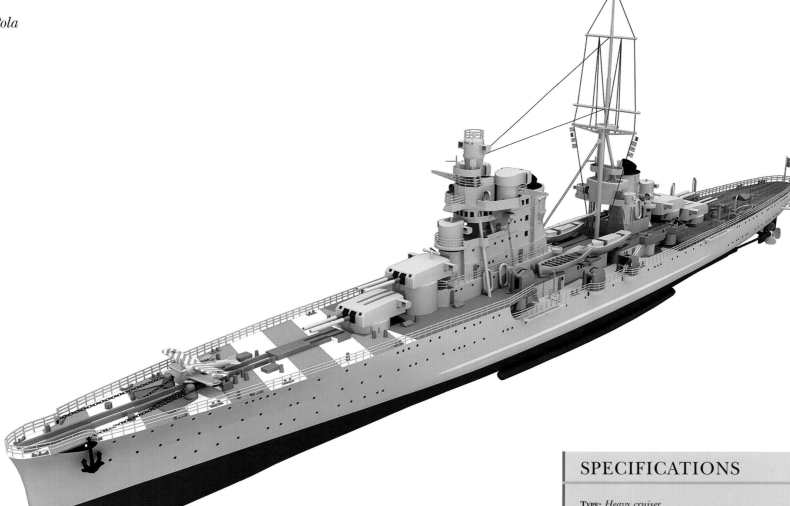

Pola

Pola was a heavy cruiser of the Italian Zara class during World War II. Experience with the preceding Trento class showed that too much had been sacrificed to obtain very high speed, and the Zaras were much better balanced designs. Armament was fairly conventional, with eight 203mm (8in) guns in four dual turrets and a secondary battery of sixteen 100mm (1.85in) guns that could serve as heavy anti-aircraft weapons or engage smaller surface targets. A mix of 40mm (1.57in) cannon and machine guns was carried for air defence. The *Pola*'s armament fit was modified in the late 1930s to incorporate more light air defence weaponry.

SPECIFICATIONS

TYPE: *Heavy cruiser*

COUNTRY OF ORIGIN: *Italy*

DISPLACEMENT: *11,730 tonnes (11,545 long tons)*

DIMENSIONS: *182.8m (600ft) Beam: 20.6m (68ft) Draught: 7.2m (24ft)*

MACHINERY: *8 boilers, 2 turbines, 2 shafts*

MAXIMUM SPEED: *32 knots (59km/h)*

ARMAMENT: *8 x 203mm/53 (8in) naval guns; 16 x 100/47mm (1.85in) OTO 1927 model guns; 6 x 40mm/49 (1.57in) Vickers-Terni machine guns; 8 x 13.2mm (0.51in) machine guns; 8 x 533mm (21in) torpedo launch tubes*

LAUNCHED: *1931*

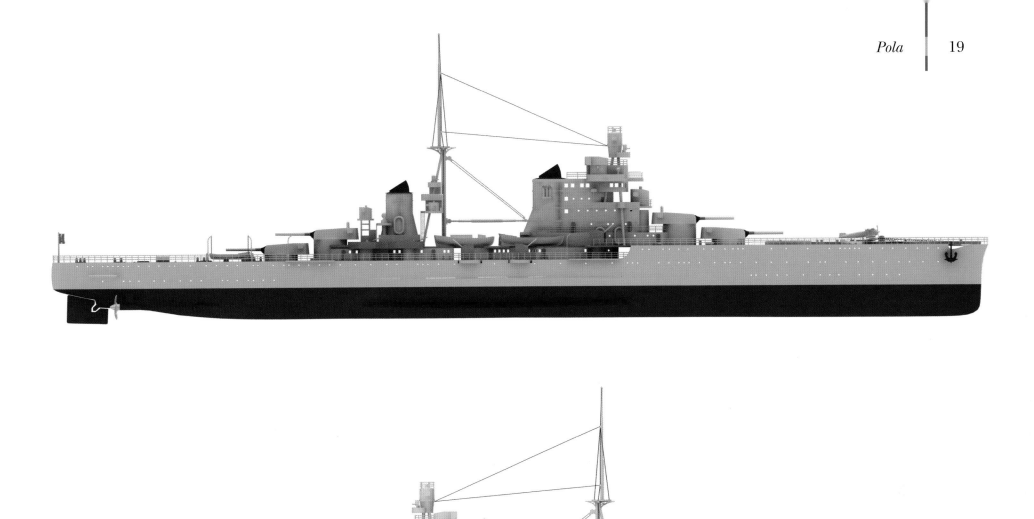

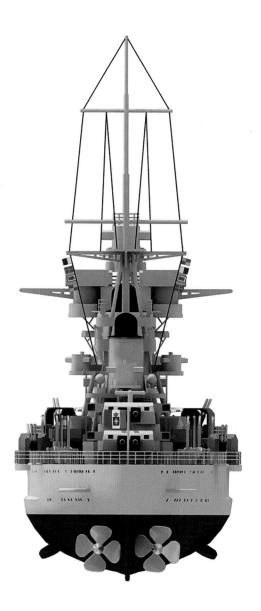

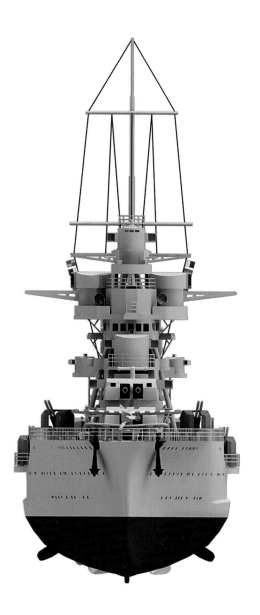

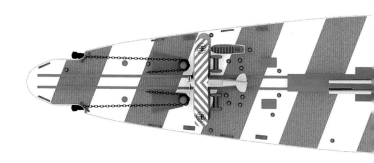

MAIN FEATURES

- Conventional heavy cruiser design
- Armament of 203mm (8in) guns capable of dealing with cruisers and lighter vessels
- Two seaplanes carried for reconnaissance

An Almost Conventional Layout
Although much of her layout was conventional, Pola differed from many other cruiser designs in that she carried an aircraft catapult forward, with a hangar for two aircraft under the forecastle.

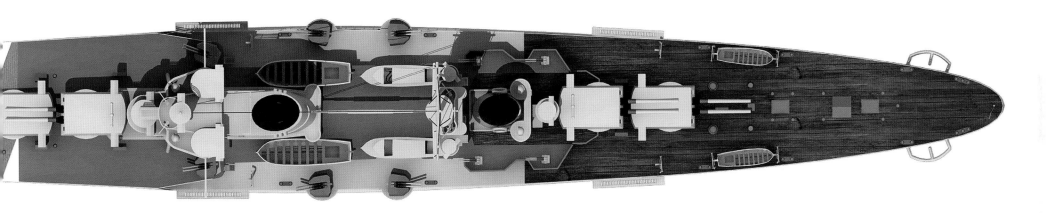

THE END OF A CLASS

Pola and two of her sister ships were sunk in the same action. On 29 March 1941, during the Battle of Matapan, torpedo aircraft from a British carrier hit Pola and brought her to a stop. Her sisters Zara and Fiume, plus some destroyers, remained to assist her. They were caught at close range, in darkness, by radar-equipped battleships. All three cruisers were quickly destroyed, with only Pola able to offer any resistance. The class's surviving member, Gorizia, was captured by the Germans upon the Italian surrender, and sunk at La Spezia in a covert operation by her former owners.

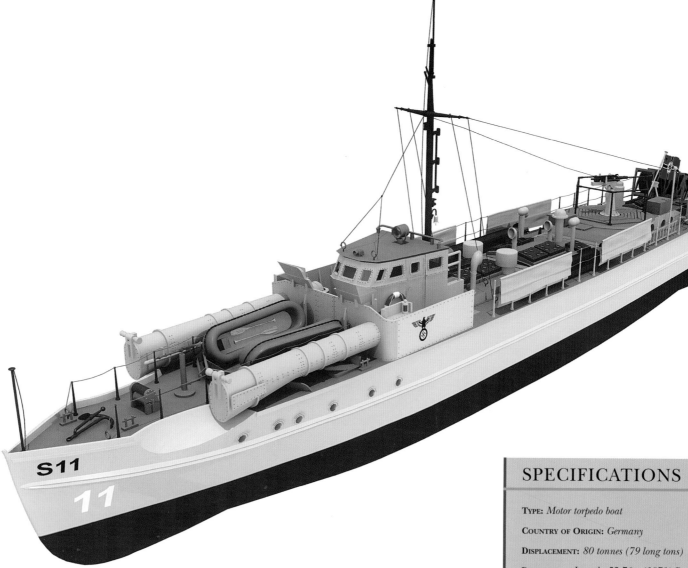

E–Boat

The vessels known to the Allies as E-boats were termed *S-boot* (*Schnellboot*, or 'Fast Boat') by their German operators. Their primary purpose was to deliver torpedoes against larger vessels. A modest gun armament allowed for other roles, however, including coastal raiding and patrol work, as well as combat against equivalent enemy vessels. The early E-boats classes were typically built around an armament of two torpedo tubes and a 20mm (0.78in) cannon. Later and larger boats had more or larger guns, and sometimes four torpedo tubes. Their gun armament provided a measure of air defence and was effective against small combatants. Nevertheless, E-boats were relatively fragile and relied primarily on their small size and high speed for defence. Operating under the cover of darkness also increased survivability.

SPECIFICATIONS

TYPE: *Motor torpedo boat*

COUNTRY OF ORIGIN: *Germany*

DISPLACEMENT: *80 tonnes (79 long tons)*

DIMENSIONS: *Length: 32.76m (107ft) Beam: 5.06m (17ft) Draught: 1.47m (5ft)*

MACHINERY: *3 x Daimler Benz twenty-cylinder diesel engines*

MAXIMUM SPEED: *43.8 knots (81km/h)*

ARMAMENT: *2 x 533mm (21in) torpedo tubes (4 torpedoes); 1 x twin 20mm (0.78in) C/30 cannon; 1 x single 20mm (0.78in) cannon; 1 x 37mm (1.46in) Flak 42 cannon*

LAUNCHED: *1939*

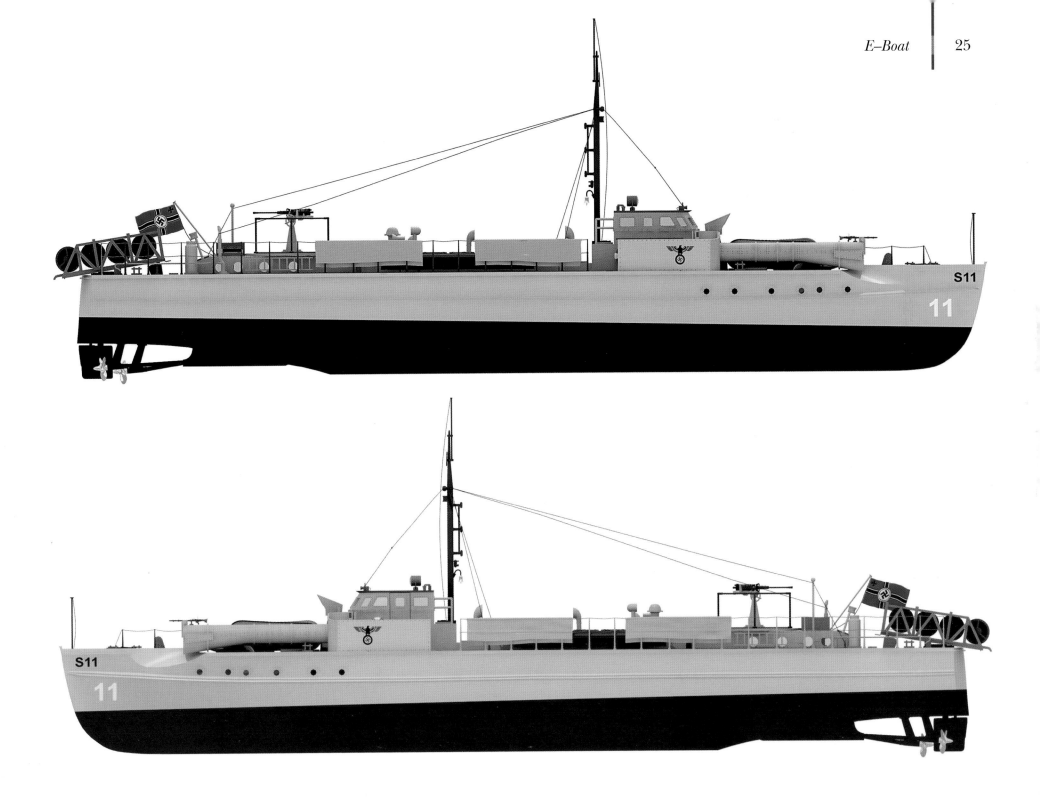

Small but Effective

E-boats were small, inexpensive combatants that were nevertheless capable of sinking merchant vessels or even warships. Once its torpedoes were expended, a boat's combat effectiveness was greatly reduced. These vessels operated primarily in the Baltic and the English Channel, often at night.

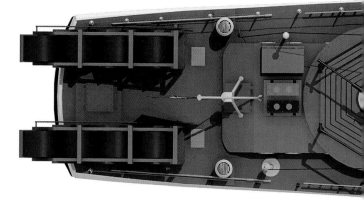

MAIN FEATURES

- High-speed fast attack craft with a relatively short operating range
- Armament of 533mm (21in) torpedoes and light guns
- Advanced rudder arrangement reduced stern wave and increased speed

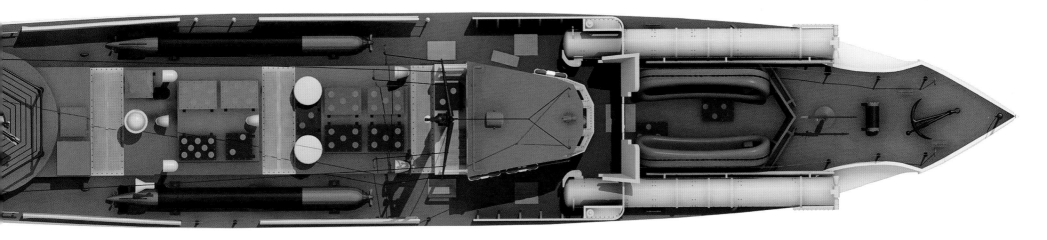

COASTAL OPERATIONS

E-boats were ideal for coastal defence and short-duration raids into the English Channel and the North Sea. Operations in the open ocean were not really feasible using such small vessels. Night actions between Allied and German small craft were not uncommon in the English Channel throughout World War II, and E-boats were at times tasked with preventing the Allies from landing reconnaissance parties and agents on the Continent. During the Normandy landings the E-boat force attempted to attack the invasion armada, but was driven off by naval escorts.

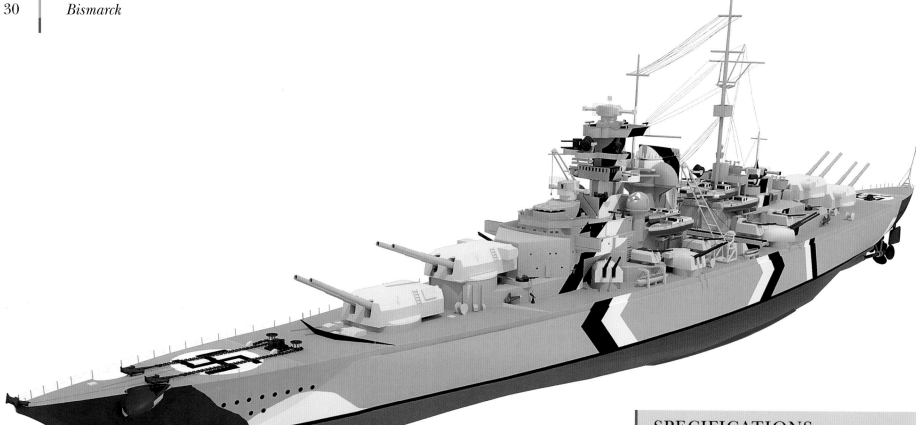

Bismarck

Bismarck and her sister ship, *Tirpitz*, were both laid down in 1936. They were the first true battleships to be built by Germany since World War I. In order to give *Bismarck* excellent protection in addition to its heavy armament and high speed, the designers greatly exceeded the vessel's official displacement of 35,000 tons that had been agreed with Britain under the London Treaty. *Bismarck* sailed on her first and only cruise in May 1941, in company with the heavy cruiser *Prinz Eugen*. Both ships slipped past Allied patrols and through the Denmark Strait. Their breakout into the Atlantic prompted the Allies to divert all available resources in a desperate attempt to prevent the heavy raiders from reaching the Atlantic convoy routes. Allied cruisers spotted the raiders in the Denmark Strait, and action eventually ensued.

SPECIFICATIONS

TYPE: *Battleship*

COUNTRY OF ORIGIN: *Germany*

DISPLACEMENT: *41,700 tonnes (41,041 long tons)*

DIMENSIONS: *Length: 251m (823ft) Beam: 36m (118ft) Draught: 9.3m (31ft)*

MACHINERY: *12 x Wagner high-pressure boilers; 3 x Blohm & Voss geared turbines*

MAXIMUM SPEED: *30.1 knots (56km/h)*

ARMAMENT: *8 x 380mm/L52 SK C/34 (15in) guns; 12 x 150mm/L55 SK-C/28 (5.9in) guns; 16 x 105mm/L65 SK-C/37/ SK-C/33 (4.1in) guns; 16 x 37mm/L83 SK-C/30 (1.5in) guns; 12 x 20mm/L65 MG C/30 (0.79in) guns; 8 x 20mm/L65 MG C/32 (0.79in) guns*

LAUNCHED: *1939*

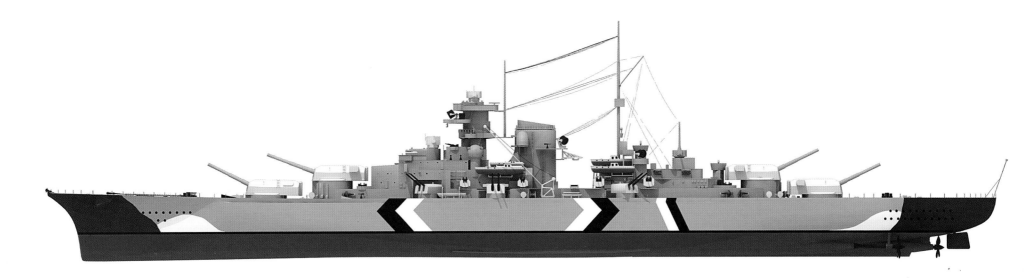

Tough and Rugged

The Bismarck class was designed to be capable of withstanding heavy fire, with extremely good armour and internal compartmentalization. A broad beam made for a stable gun platform, augmented by radar and excellent optical rangefinding equipment.

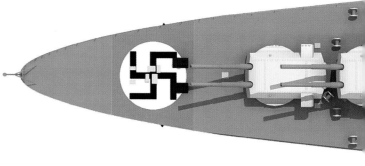

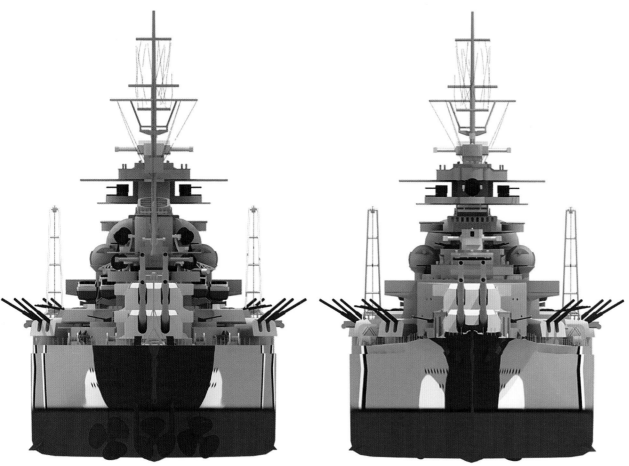

MAIN FEATURES

- Heavily protected fast battleship design
- Main armament of eight 380mm (15in) guns
- 'Atlantic Bow' designed to cope with heavy swell in the open ocean

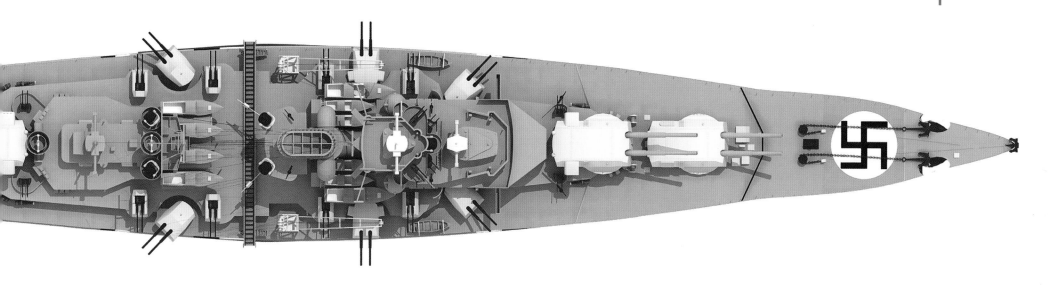

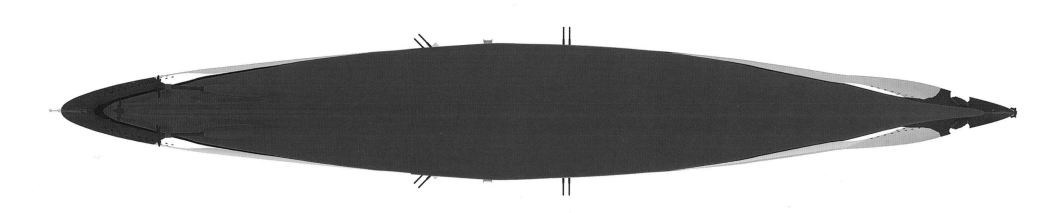

BATTLE IN THE STRAIT

Fast battleships such as Bismarck *were ideal for deployment as heavy raiders. Their big guns could quickly sink any convoy escorts and wreak havoc among the defenceless merchants, while their speed allowed them to evade pursuit by enemy capital ships. Despite this,* Bismarck *went down on her maiden mission under these very circumstances, in the Denmark Strait on 24 May 1941. After a successful engagement in which the British battlecruiser HMS* Hood *was sunk,* Bismarck *almost evaded her pursuers. Slowed by torpedo-bomber attacks, which jammed her rudder, she was brought to action by an overwhelming force of cruisers and capital ships, and fought against impossible odds until she was pounded to a wreck. Some sources state that she was scuttled by her crew when she could no longer fight; others claim she was finished off by torpedoes. The accompanying German cruiser* Prinz Eugen *slipped away, but was forced to return to port with engine trouble.*

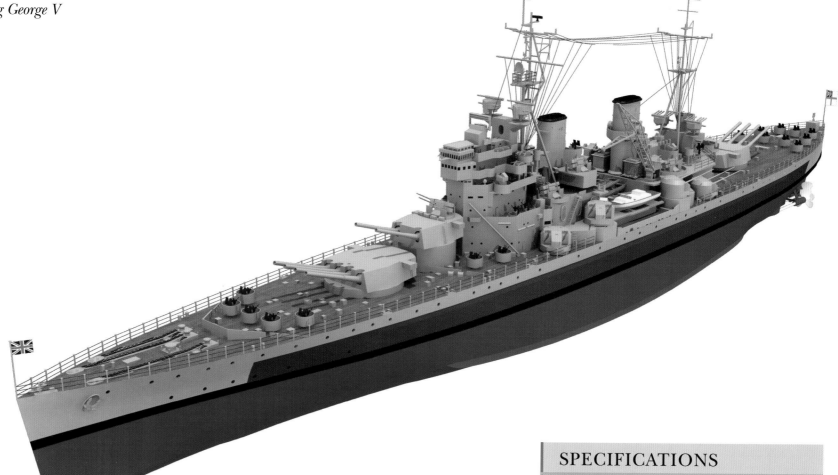

King George V

The King George V class battleships were specialist vessels designed to engage and destroy any enemy surface combatant. As such they mounted no anti-submarine weapons, but carried what was at the time considered an adequate anti-aircraft armament. This was subsequently upgraded as a result of wartime experience. The King George V class was designed to meet the limitations of the London Treaty, and was to displace 35,000 tons. The treaty lapsed during construction, however, and various modifications were made, resulting in a greater displacement. Armament was conventional in size but not layout, in that it was intended to bring the most guns to bear while pursuing or steaming towards an opponent, rather than offering balanced all-round firepower.

SPECIFICATIONS

Type: *Battleship*

Country of Origin: *United Kingdom*

Displacement: *42,877 tonnes (42,200 long tons)*

Dimensions: *Length: 227m (745ft) Beam: 31m (102ft) Draught: 9.9m (32ft)*

Machinery: *8 x Admiralty three-drum small-tube boilers with superheaters; 4 x Parsons single-reduction geared turbines*

Maximum Speed: *28 knots (52km/h)*

Armament: *10 x BL 360mm (14in) Mk VII guns; 16 x QF 133mm (5¼-in) Mk I guns; 64 x 40mm (2-pounder) 'pom-pom' guns (1941)*

Launched: *1939*

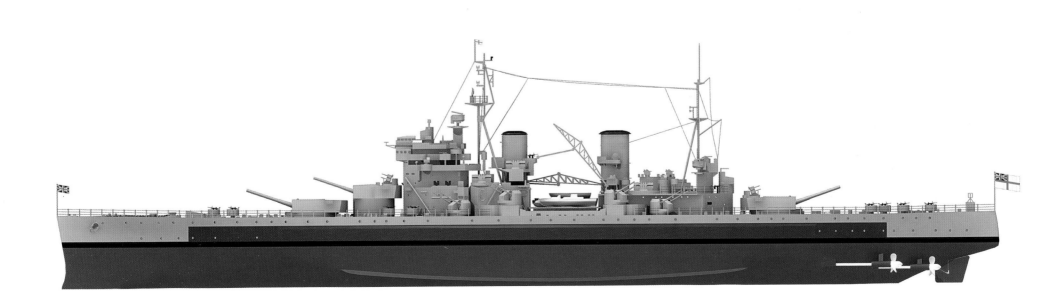

Quadruple Turrets

Six 360mm (14in) guns were mounted forward, in a quadruple turret with a dual turret superfiring it. A second quadruple turret was mounted aft and contained the same calibre weapons. These weapon mounts suffered from persistent technical problems in all ships of the class. Although the quadruple turrets offered theoretical advantages in terms of ammunition handling and armour protection, in practice they were sufficiently troublesome to affect combat efficiency.

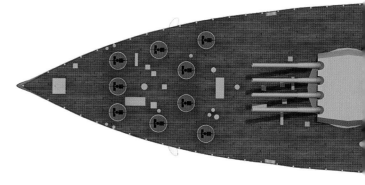

MAIN FEATURES

- Well-armoured battleship, capable of 28 knots
- Heavy main armament with most guns concentrated forward
- Four seaplanes originally carried for reconnaissance; removed to make room for upgraded air-defence armament

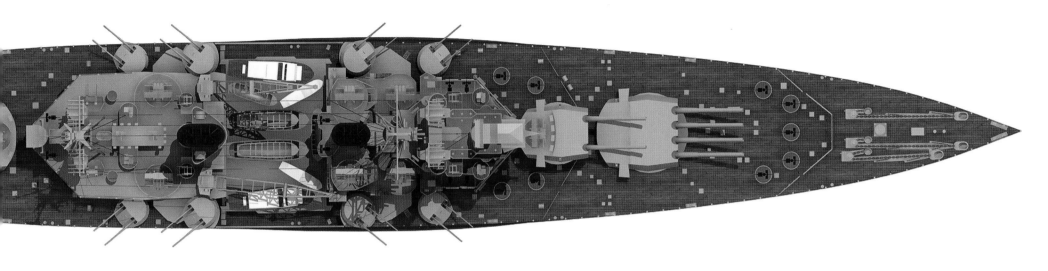

WIDE-RANGING SERVICE

HMS King George V *was involved in the pursuit of the* Bismarck *in the Denmark Strait in May 1941, firing more than 300 heavy shells at the German battleship. She also provided heavy cover for convoys and shelled enemy shore positions in the Mediterranean, and served as VIP transport for British Prime Minister Winston Churchill. Her wartime role continued right up to the conflict's end: she was present at the Japanese surrender ceremony that ended World War II.*

Snowberry

The Flower class of corvettes of which HMCS *Snowberry* was a part was hurriedly designed and put into production to provide sufficient antisubmarine escorts at the beginning of World War II. Based on a civilian whaling-ship hull, early examples were considerably modified during construction and some members of the class differed significantly from others. General-purpose armament consisted of a single 101.6mm (4in) gun, plus machine guns, but these vessels were never intended to engage other surface combatants; they were specialist ships rushed into production to counter the German U-boat menace to the Atlantic and other convoy routes. For this purpose the Flower class carried depth charges and, later in World War II, Hedgehog anti-submarine mortars.

SPECIFICATIONS

TYPE: *Corvette*

COUNTRY OF ORIGIN: *Canada*

DISPLACEMENT: *940 tonnes (925 long tons)*

DIMENSIONS: *Length: 62.48m (205ft) Beam: 10.06m (33ft) Draught: 3.51m (12ft)*

MACHINERY: *2 x fire tube Scotch boilers; 1 x 4-cycle triple-expansion reciprocating steam engine; single shaft*

MAXIMUM SPEED: *16 knots (30km/h)*

ARMAMENT: *1 x BL 101.6mm (4in) Mk.IX gun; 2 x 50 cal. machine gun (twin); 2 x Lewis 7.69mm (.303in) machine gun (twin); 2 x Mk.II depth charge throwers; 2 x depth charge rails with 40 depth charges*

LAUNCHED: *1940*

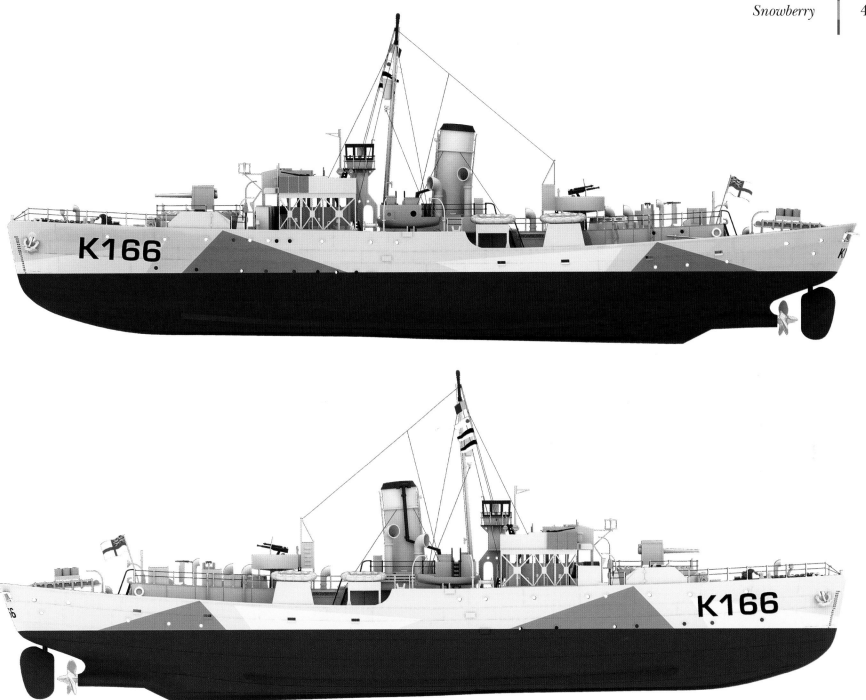

Excellent Seaworthiness

The whaling-vessel hull used for Snowberry and similar corvettes was unglamorous, but extremely seaworthy. These little vessels gave good service on the hazardous convoy routes during World War II, freeing more potent warships for other duties. Snowberry was intended for the Royal Navy, but was taken up by the Royal Canadian Navy for wartime service instead. She was returned to the Royal Navy at the end of the war, but was surplus to requirements in peacetime and was quickly retired.

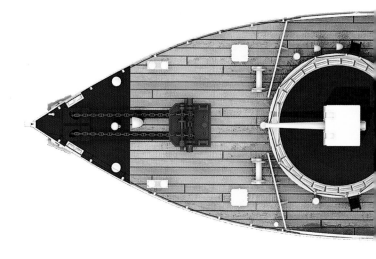

MAIN FEATURES

- Modest 16-knot performance, adequate for escort work
- Anti-submarine armament of 40–72 depth charges (and anti-submarine mortar in some cases)
- Range of 3500 nautical miles at 12 knots

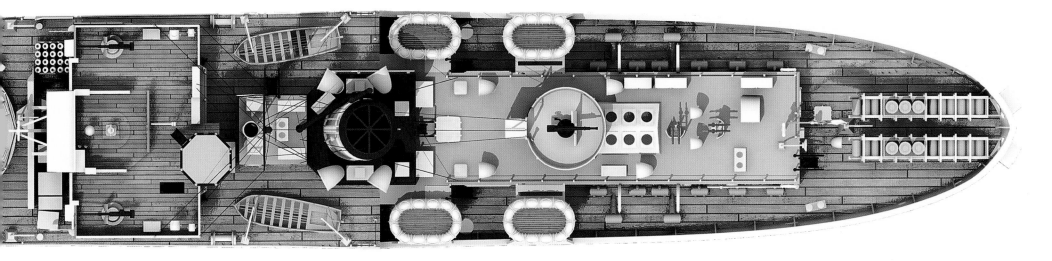

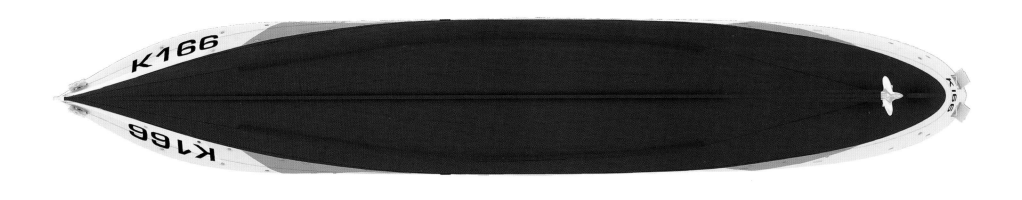

ANTI-SUBMARINE ROLE

Small escorts such as Snowberry *and others of the Flower class, such as* Sackville *pictured here, were optimized for anti-submarine work. Their light guns could easily deal with a surfaced submarine, but would be little use against a major warship. In 1943, HMCS* Snowberry *was part of a sub-hunting group that depth-charged and sank* U-536.

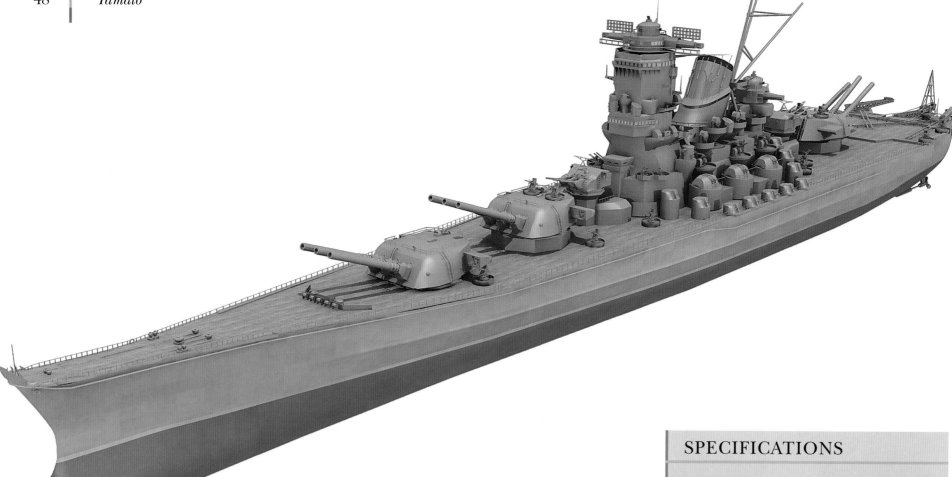

Yamato

Yamato was the lead ship of her class, the largest, heaviest and most heavily armed battleships ever built. Built around a main battery of nine 460mm (18.1in) guns, the Yamato class carried a secondary armament of twelve 155mm (6.1in) and twelve 127mm (5in) guns – more or less equivalent to two light cruisers. A heavy anti-aircraft armament was also shipped, along with catapults for seven aircraft. *Yamato* served as the Japanese flagship at the Battle of Midway, but did not play much part in what was essentially a carrier action. Similarly, she was unable to get into action at the Battle of the Philippine Sea. At the 1944 Battle of Leyte Gulf, *Yamato* was damaged and her sister ship *Musashi* was sunk, both by air attack.

SPECIFICATIONS

TYPE: *Battleship*

COUNTRY OF ORIGIN: *Japan*

DISPLACEMENT: *65,027 tonnes (64,000 long tons)*

DIMENSIONS: *Length: 256m (840ft) Beam: 36.9m (121ft) Draught: 11m (36ft)*

MACHINERY: *12 x Kampon boilers, driving 4 x steam turbines*

MAXIMUM SPEED: *27 knots (50km/h)*

ARMAMENT: *9 x 460mm (18.1in) guns; 12 x 155mm (6.1in) guns; 12 x 127mm (5in) guns*

LAUNCHED: *1940*

Heavy Armour Protection

Built in great secrecy, Yamato and other vessels of her class incorporated very heavy armour protection. Indeed, Yamato's main guns were so large that a heavy-lift ship had to be specially built to carry them and their mountings to the shipyard. The weight of each triple turret was more than 2500 tonnes. A huge hull was required to support such enormous weapons.

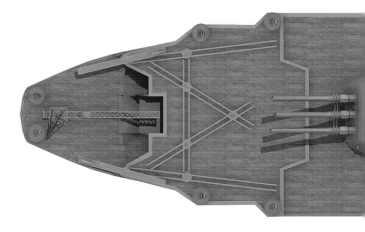

MAIN FEATURES

- Huge superbattleship capable of 27 knots
- Main armament of 460mm (18.1in) guns capable of sinking anything afloat
- Third ship of the class converted to an aircraft carrier

TORPEDO HAZARD

Yamato and her sisters were designed to withstand hits from their own main armament, which was significantly heavier than anything mounted by a foreign vessel. Torpedo protection proved less effective than had been hoped, but even so it took between nine and thirteen torpedoes, plus six bombs, to sink *Yamato* on 7 April 1945. As the Allies began their assault on Okinawa, *Yamato* sortied on what was envisaged from the start as a death ride. With only enough fuel available for a one-way trip, she had orders to get in among the invasion fleet and do as much damage as possible, then beach herself and act as a shore battery. The sortie was intercepted by aircraft well short of the fleet; *Yamato* was sunk without firing a shot at the Allied fleet.

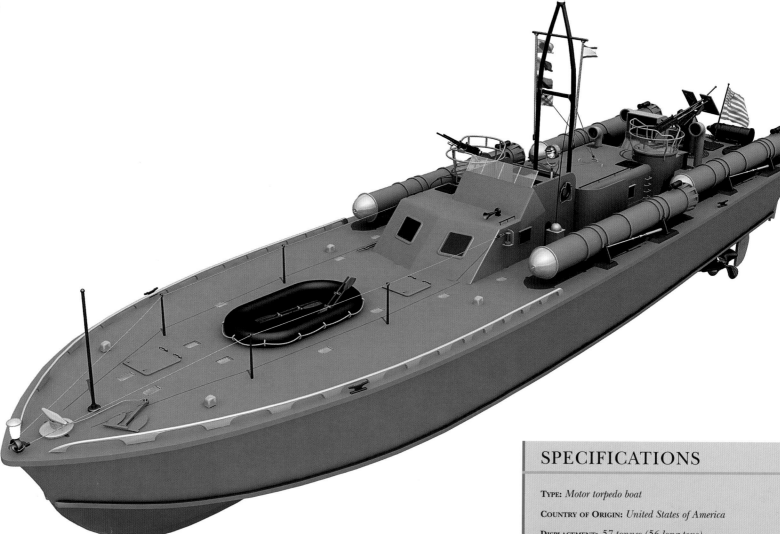

PT-109

PT-109 was to become the most famous example of the large PT-103 class of fast torpedo-armed small craft, captained as it was by future US President John F. Kennedy. The US Navy became interested in such vessels in the late 1930s, when other navies began building them in significant numbers. A variety of designs were used during World War II, with most classes evolving as a result of experience in combat. The primary armament of the PT boat was its torpedoes; four 533mm (21in) weapons in tubes on most classes. A light gun armament, initially comprising machine guns, was fitted. This gradually increased as the war went on and the PT boat force became increasingly involved in close-range actions against Japanese gunboats and transport barges operating in the Pacific island groups. Late-war boats carried 20mm (0.78in) to 40mm (1.57in) cannon, plus mortars and rocket launchers.

SPECIFICATIONS

TYPE: *Motor torpedo boat*

COUNTRY OF ORIGIN: *United States of America*

DISPLACEMENT: *57 tonnes (56 long tons)*

DIMENSIONS: *Length: 24m (79ft) Beam: 6.3m (21ft) Draught: 1.07m (4ft)*

MACHINERY: *3 x 12-cylinder Packard gasoline engines*

MAXIMUM SPEED: *41 knots (76km/h)*

ARMAMENT: *4 x 533mm (21in) torpedo tubes (four Mark VIII torpedoes); 1 x 20mm (0.78in) cannon, 4 x 12.7mm (.5in) machine guns; 1 x 37mm (1.46in) anti-tank gun*

LAUNCHED: *1920*

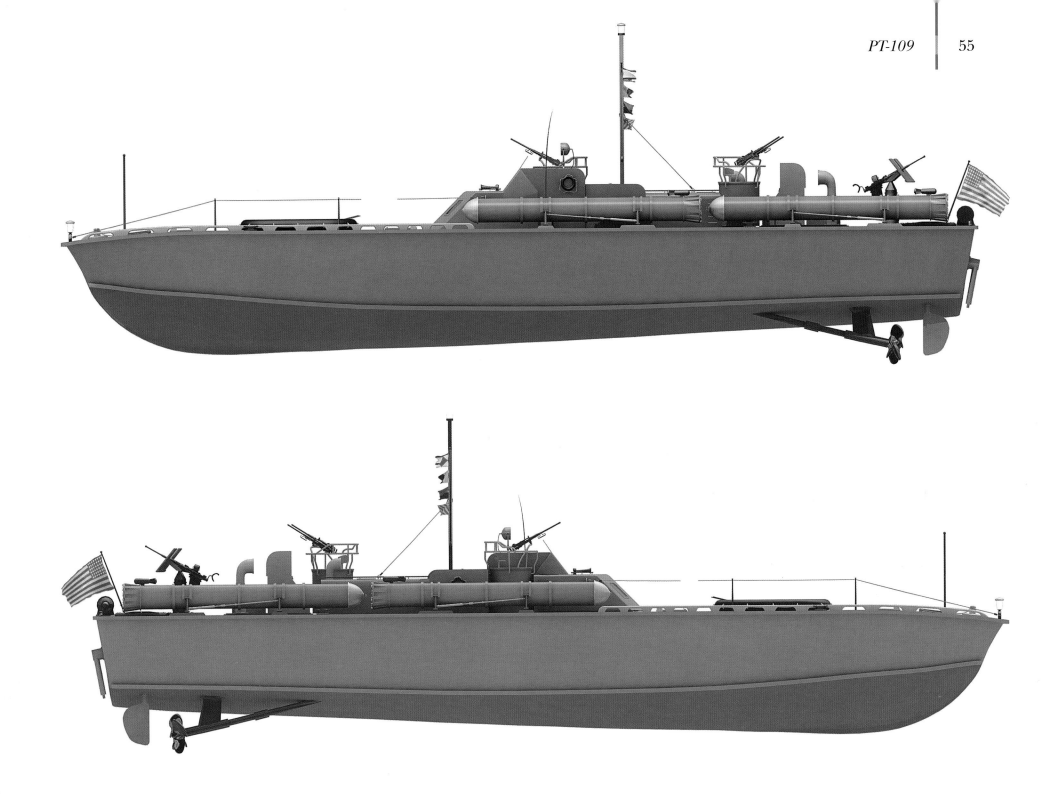

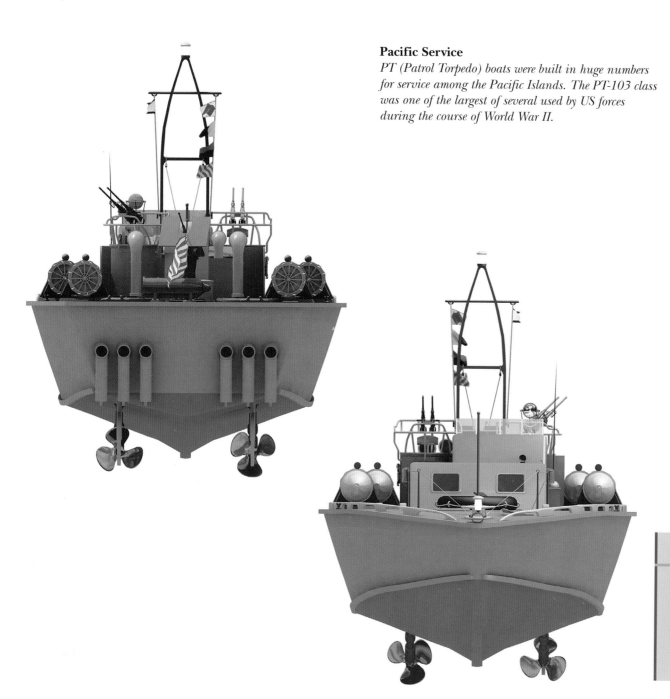

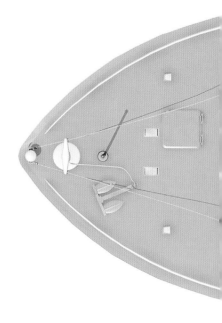

Pacific Service

PT (Patrol Torpedo) boats were built in huge numbers for service among the Pacific Islands. The PT-103 class was one of the largest of several used by US forces during the course of World War II.

MAIN FEATURES

- Small expendable attack craft
- Main armament of torpedoes was effective against most ships
- Top speed of 41 knots for target approach and escape

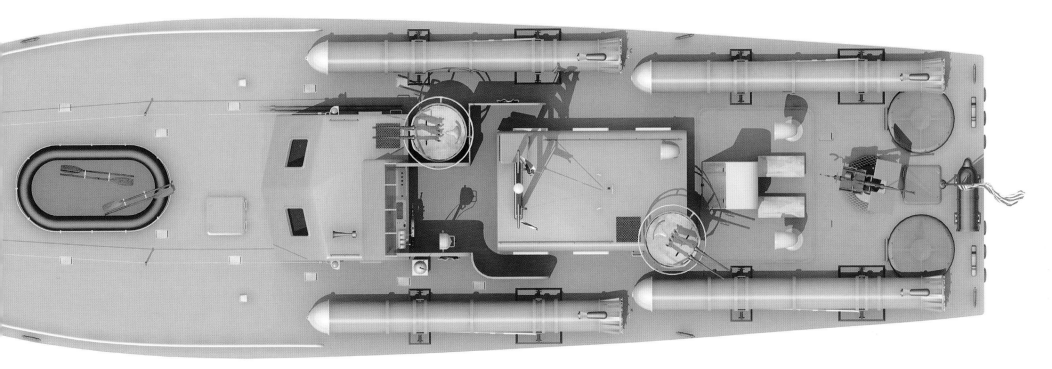

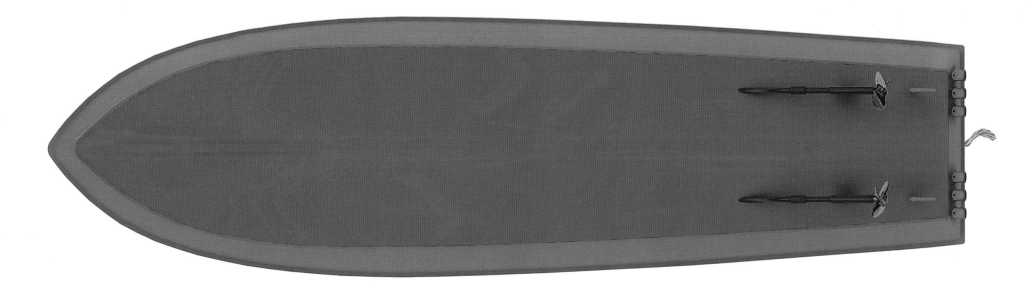

AIR-ATTACK SURVIVAL

Air attack was a constant threat to PT boats. The twin 12.7mm (0.5in) machine-gun mounts on PT-180, another example of the PT-103 class, offered at least some measure of defensive capability. High speed and evasion offered the best hope of surviving an air attack.

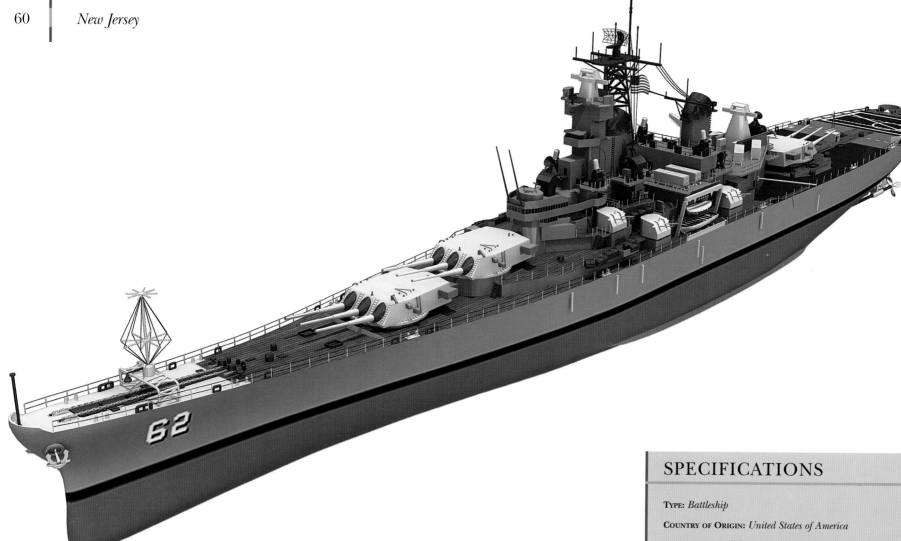

New Jersey

USS *New Jersey* was a fast battleship of the Iowa class, designed in the late 1930s. The class's primary role was domination of the seas, using a heavy gun armament to destroy any surface threat. The changing nature of warfare, however, caused this role to be altered at times. Most notably, *New Jersey* was reconfigured as a 'missile battleship', carrying a heavy missile armament in addition to her guns. The original main battery of nine 406mm (16in) guns was retained, but was eventually augmented with cruise missiles. Similarly the secondary battery of 127mm (5in) guns was never entirely removed, but came to include anti-ship and anti-air missiles. A lighter anti-air fit later included 20mm (0.78in) close-in weapon systems.

SPECIFICATIONS

TYPE: *Battleship*

COUNTRY OF ORIGIN: *United States of America*

DISPLACEMENT: *45,722 tonnes (45,000 long tons)*

DIMENSIONS: *270.5m (887ft) Beam: 33m (108ft) Draught: 8.8m (29ft)*

MACHINERY: *4 x General Electric cross-compound steam turbine engines*

MAXIMUM SPEED: *31 knots (57km/h)*

ARMAMENT: *9 x 406mm (16in)/50 cal. Mark 7 guns; 20 x 127mm (5in)/38 cal. Mark 12 guns*

LAUNCHED: *1942*

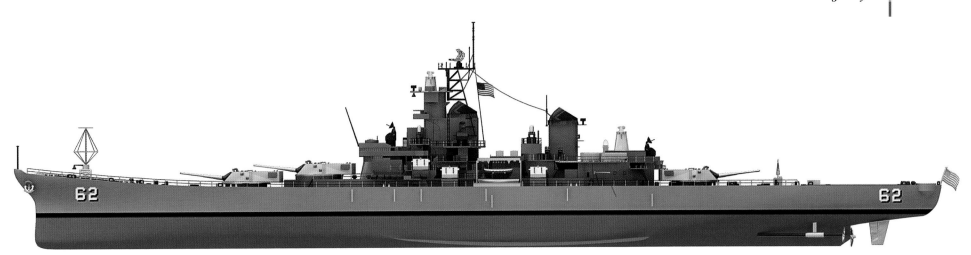

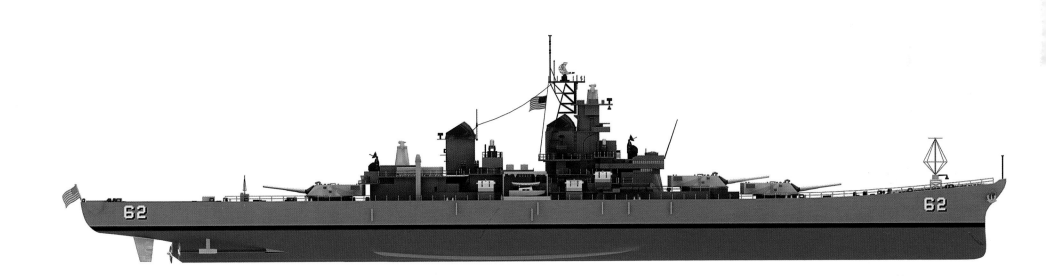

Straightforward Reconfiguration

Although New Jersey *was designed long before naval helicopters or missile systems were envisaged, her large hull made it relatively simple to fit additional systems. Tomahawk missile container-launchers take up little space compared to triple 406mm (16in) gun turrets and their associated machinery.*

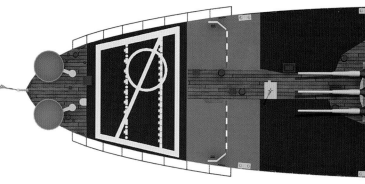

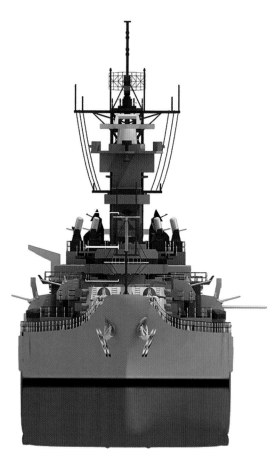

MAIN FEATURES

- Heavily armoured fast battleship capable of 33 knots

- Armament upgraded to incorporate a heavy missile complement

- Helicopter pad added aft, replacing reconnaissance floatplanes

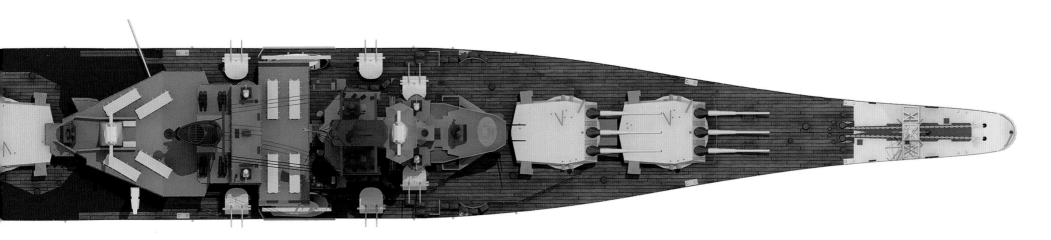

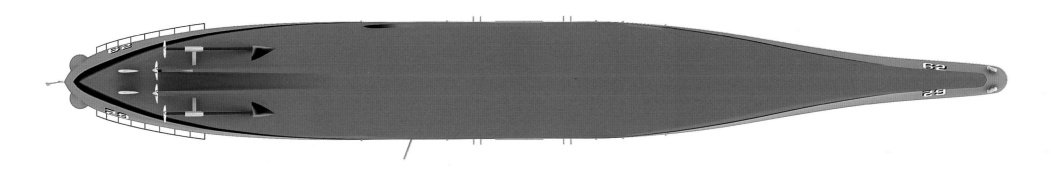

MISSILE BATTLESHIP

Although dwarfed by the giant main gun turrets, the missile containers and Phalanx close-in weapon systems fitted on New Jersey's superstructure allowed her to remain a potent naval asset more than half a century after she was designed. Her final period of service, as a missile battleship, began in 1982. In this role she launched cruise missiles and provided gunfire support, before returning to the 'mothball fleet' in 1991. She has since been converted to a museum ship.

Yorktown

USS *Yorktown* (CV-10), an aircraft carrier of the Essex class, was launched on 21 January 1943. Laid down as USS *Bon Homme Richard*, she was renamed during construction when *Yorktown* (CV-5) was sunk at the Battle of Midway. The Essex class was developed from the preceding Yorktown class and incorporated lessons learned with those ships, as well as new technologies, including more powerful machinery. The Essex class carried a battery of twelve 127mm (5in) guns, primarily as heavy anti-aircraft weapons, plus an extensive fit of 40mm (1.57in) and 20mm (0.78in) guns. The air group consisted of 36 fighters, 37 dive-bombers and 18 torpedo-bombers, and comprised the carrier's primary means of both attack and defence.

SPECIFICATIONS

TYPE: *Aircraft carrier*

COUNTRY OF ORIGIN: *United States of America*

DISPLACEMENT: *31,294 tonnes (30,800 long tons)*

DIMENSIONS: *Length: 266m (873ft) Beam: 45m (148ft) Draught: 10.41m (34ft)*

MACHINERY: *8 x boilers; 4 x Westinghouse geared steam turbines; 4 x shafts*

MAXIMUM SPEED: *33 knots (61km/h)*

ARMAMENT: *Aircraft: 90–100. Weapons: 4 x twin 127 mm (5in)/38 cal. guns; 4 x single 127 mm (5in)/38 cal. guns; 8 x quadruple 40mm (1.57in) 56 cal. guns; 46 x single 20mm (0.78in) 78 cal. guns*

LAUNCHED: *1943*

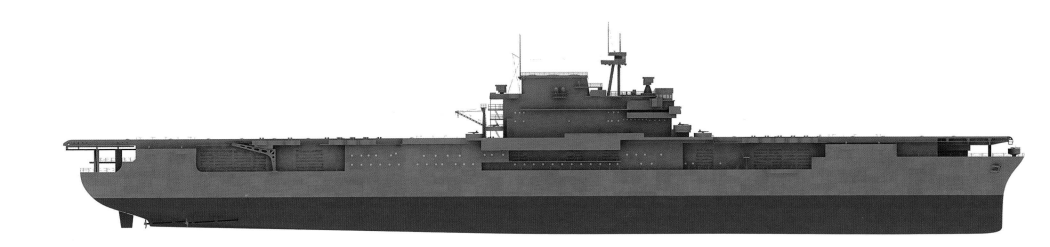

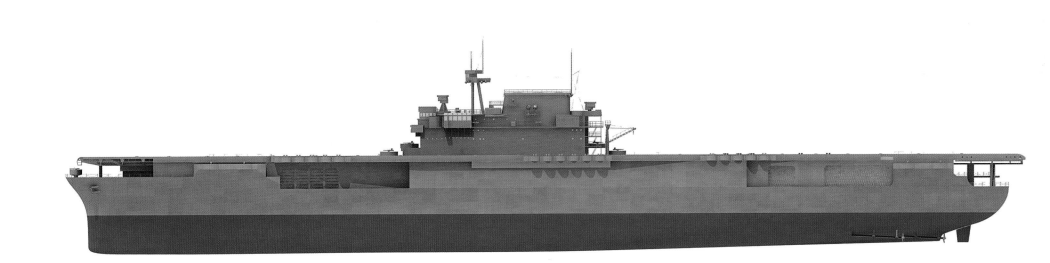

Flight Deck Superstructure

USS Yorktown*'s flight deck and hangars were built on the main hull as a superstructure. The ship's vital machinery was protected by an armoured flight deck and a second armoured deck at the hangar level.* Yorktown *served in the Pacific theatre during World War II, participating in the 'island-hopping' campaigns of the Allied advance.*

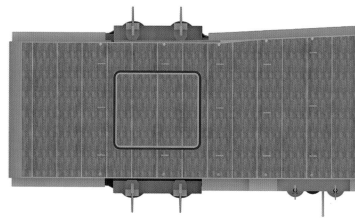

MAIN FEATURES

- Fast aircraft carrier capable of 32 knots
- Air group of capable of attacking land and sea targets
- Armoured flight deck

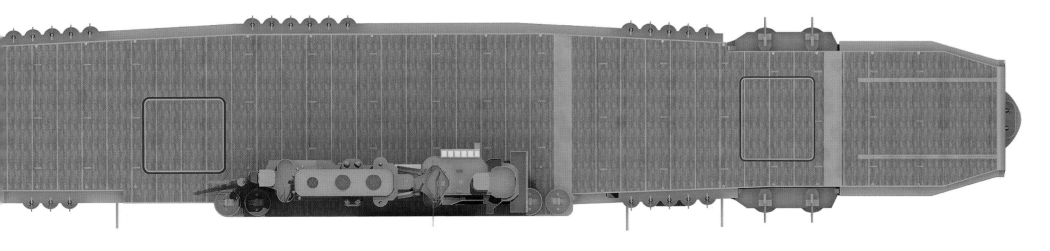

MULTIPLE ROLES

After World War II, Yorktown *spent several years in reserve before recommissioning. She was adapted to carry jet fighters as an attack carrier and was later redesignated as an anti-submarine carrier. She served in this capacity during the Vietnam War and as a recovery ship for the Apollo 8 astronauts, before finally decommissioning in 1975.*

Vosper MTB

Motor torpedo boats (MTBs) were operated by the Royal Navy Coastal Forces during World War II. A variety of designs was used, evolving as a result of experience and new technology throughout the war. Vosper Ltd provided many of these boats, starting with a 48-knot vessel bought by the Royal Navy in 1937. This boat had the distinction of being the fastest vessel operated by the Royal Navy during the war. Early Vosper torpedo boats were armed with two torpedoes and two to four machine guns, with some examples also carrying depth charges. As the war progressed a standard design emerged, designated Vosper Type I. This boat carried four torpedoes and a 20mm (0.78in) cannon, plus usually two machine guns. Modified versions of this general class appeared throughout the war.

SPECIFICATIONS

Type: *Motor torpedo boat*

Country of Origin: *United Kingdom*

Displacement: *47 tonnes (46 long tons)*

Dimensions: *Length: 22m (73ft)*

Machinery: *3 Packard 12M engines*

Maximum Speed: *40 knots (74km/h)*

Armament: *Four 457 mm (18in) torpedo tubes; 1 x Oerlikon 20mm (0.78in) cannon; 2 x 7.69mm (0.303in) Vickers K machine guns*

Launched: *1943*

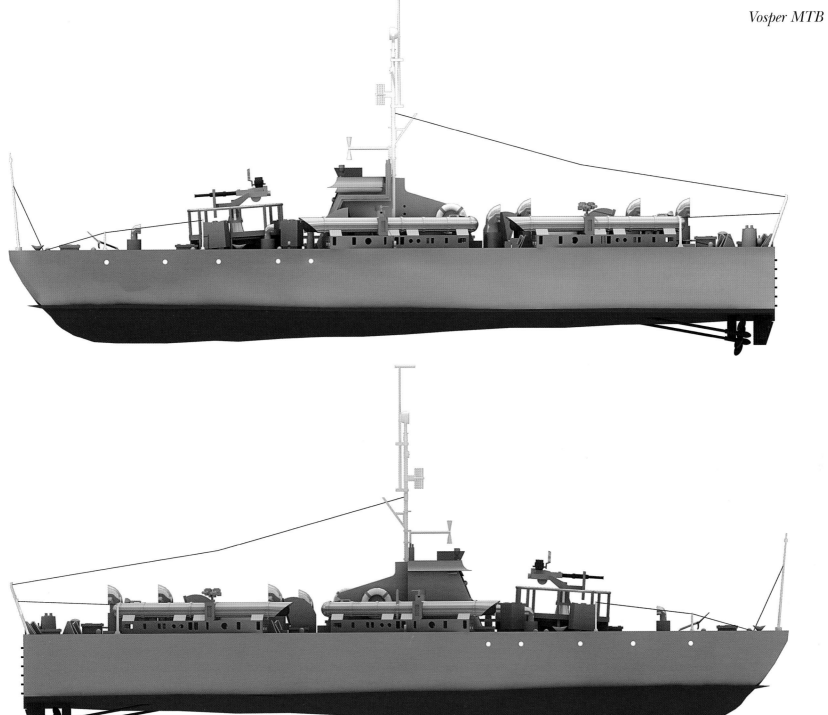

Powerful Weaponry

The four torpedoes in their offset launchers gave British MTBs a powerful weapon against larger vessels, assuming the boat could survive long enough to reach launching distance. For this reason the overall design was as light as possible, as speed and agility were the only real defence these small vessels possessed.

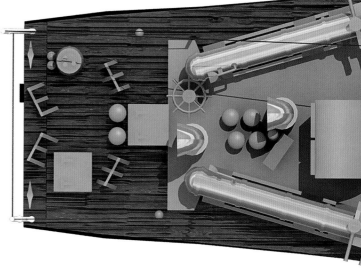

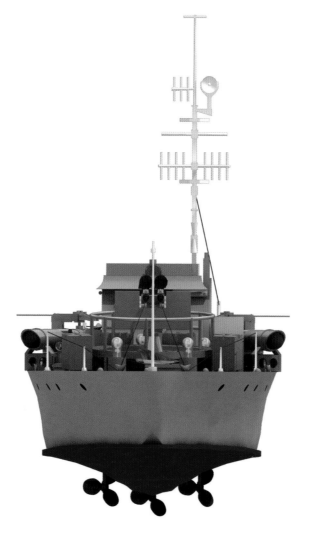

MAIN FEATURES

- Small fast attack craft with short operating range
- Torpedo armament backed up by light guns
- Many small variations found between individual vessels

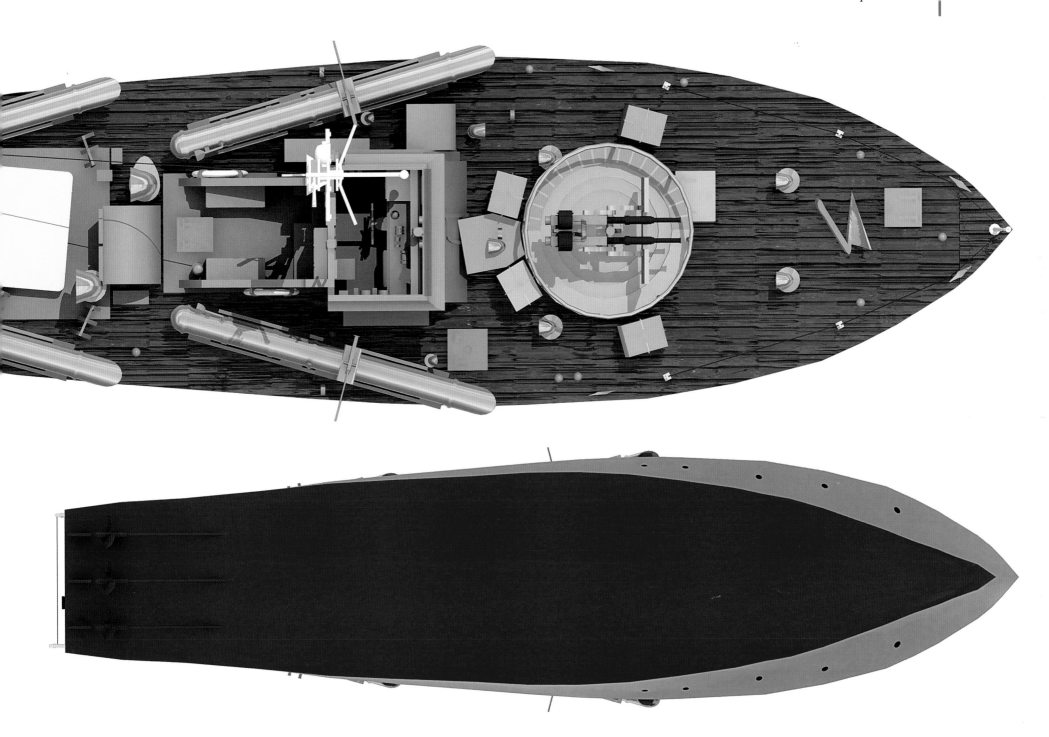

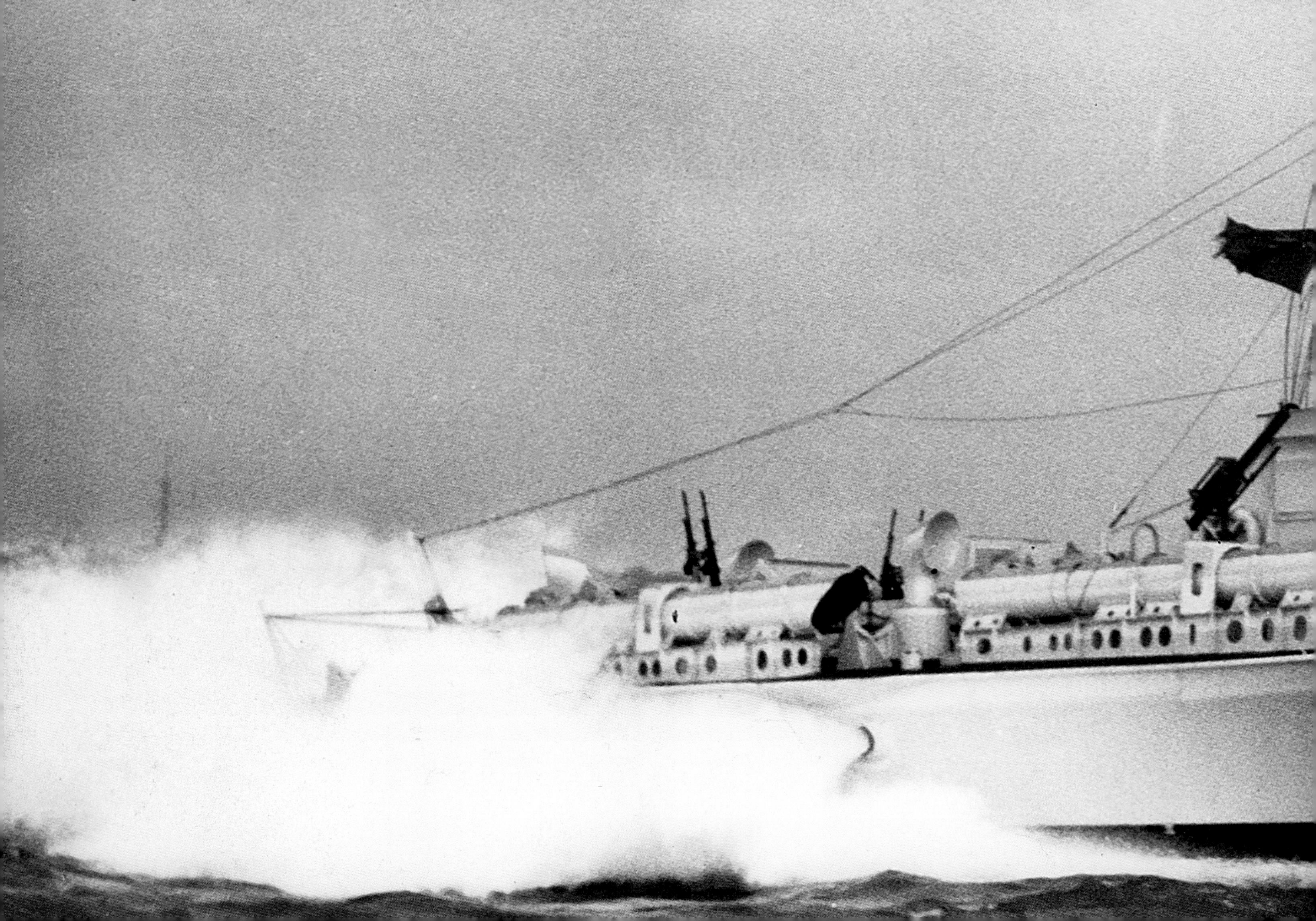

DEFENDING THE COAST

MTB 385 *was a Vosper 22m (73ft) type armed with four torpedo tubes, four machine guns, two 20mm (0.78in) cannon and two depth charges. Some later boats of the same type carried a six-pounder (57mm) gun instead of two of the torpedo tubes. This was because, although motor gun boats (MGBs) existed to counter the E-boat threat, it was felt that a more balanced MBT design was desirable, enabling the coastal forces to deal with Germany's E-boats more effectively.*

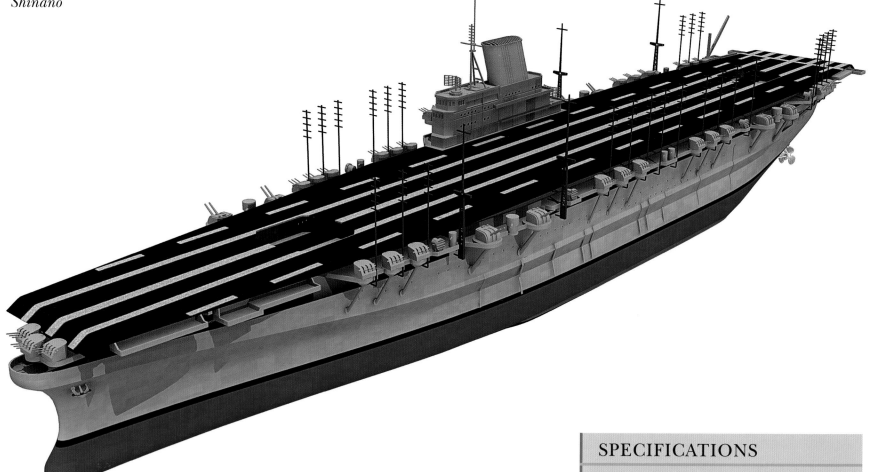

Shinano

Shinano started out as a huge battleship of the Yamato class, but was converted during building into a carrier to offset Japanese losses taken at the Battle of Midway in 1941. She retained some of her battleship-grade armour, although the main belt was thinned considerably. An armoured deck offered protection from the largest bombs then in use by the US carrier forces. *Shinano* was not meant to be a frontline 'fighting carrier', but instead to function as a support ship, conveying supplies and reserve aircraft for other members of the carrier force. Armament included sixteen 127mm (5in) guns and more than 100 25mm (0.98mm) cannon for air defence, plus rocket launchers. Like all carriers, however, *Shinano* was intended to engage with her aircraft, rather than her own weapons. Despite her size, her hangar capacity was only about 70 aircraft.

SPECIFICATIONS

TYPE: *Aircraft carrier*

COUNTRY OF ORIGIN: *Japan*

DISPLACEMENT: *63,000 tonnes (62,005 long tons)*

DIMENSIONS: *266m (873ft) Beam: 36.3m (119ft) Draught: 40m (131ft)*

MACHINERY: *4 x geared steam turbines; 12 x Kampon oil-fired boilers; 4 x shafts*

MAXIMUM SPEED: *27 knots (50km/h)*

ARMAMENT: *Aircraft: 18. Weapons: 16 x 127mm (5in) dual-purpose guns; 145 x 25mm (0.98in) anti-aircraft guns; 12 x 28-barreled 127mm (5in) anti-aircraft rocket launchers*

LAUNCHED: *1940*

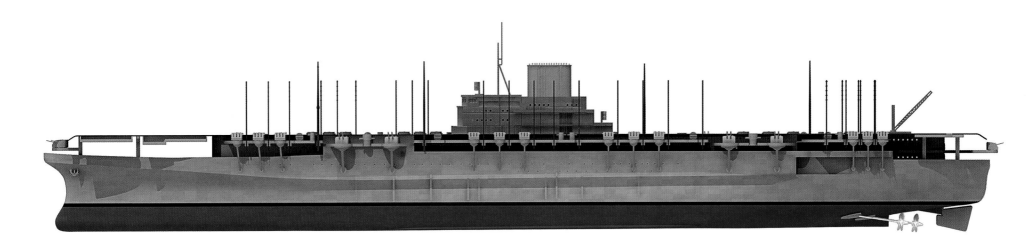

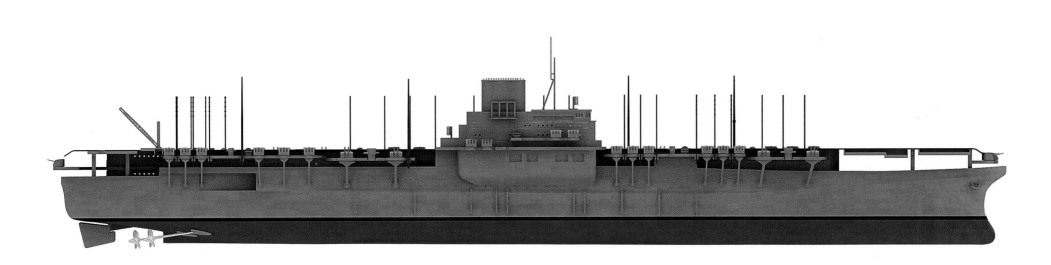

Formidable Armament

Commissioned in November 1944 (although still not complete), Shinano *was the largest aircraft carrier ever built until the USS* Enterprise *was launched in 1960, and was converted in secret. She mounted a formidable anti-aircraft armament and possessed an armoured flight deck to protect her from bombing attacks. She also retained much of her battleship armour, although the main belt was significantly lightened.*

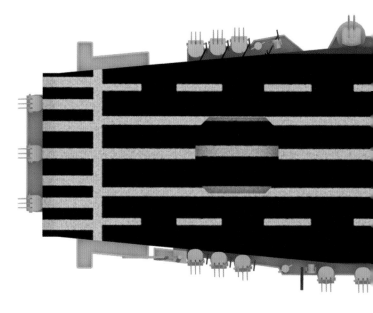

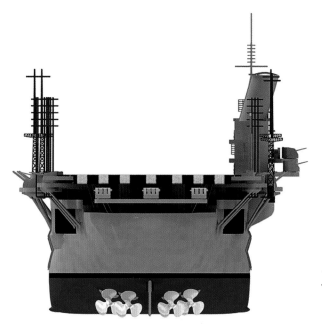

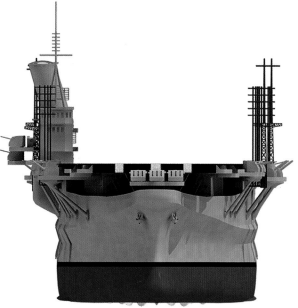

MAIN FEATURES

- Aircraft carrier converted from superbattleship
- Capable of operating up to 70 aircraft
- Aircraft repair facility carried aboard

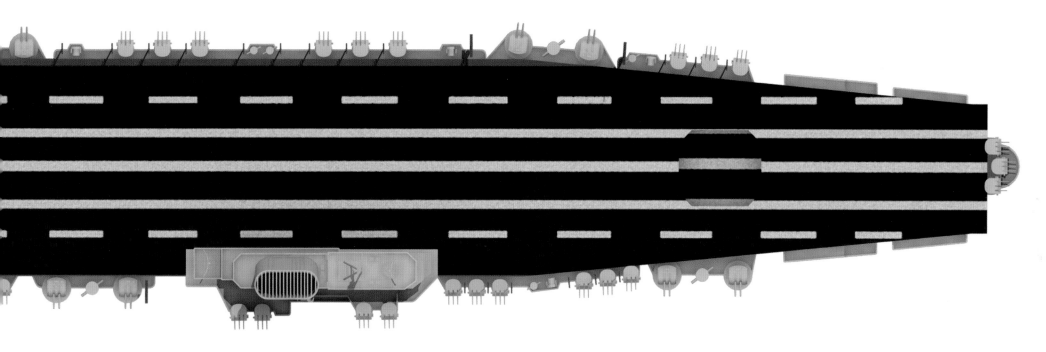

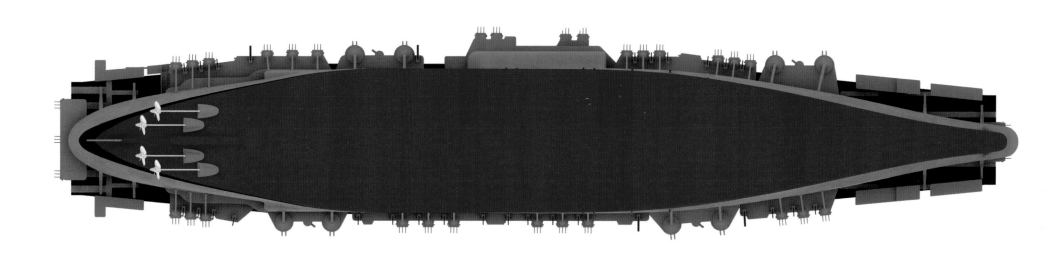

SUBMARINE ATTACK

The danger of air attack prompted the decision to finish fitting out Shinano at the port of Kure, but putting to sea exposed her to US submarines. On the way to Kure, Shinano was torpedoed by USS Archerfish. With some of her watertight compartments not yet fitted with doors and a crew inadequately trained in damage-control procedures, Shinano suffered gradually increasing flooding and sank after several hours, only ten days after her commissioning. She was the largest warship ever sunk by submarine attack. Had her watertight compartmentalization been complete, she may well have survived the damage.

Nanuchka Class

The Nanuchka class are large missile boats ('rocket cutters', in Russian parlance) built for coastal defence and sea denial operations in areas close to a home port. They have a greater endurance and operating range than smaller missile boat classes, but are not suitable for open-ocean operations because they are poor sea boats. Despite this, the Nanuchka class has at times operated quite far from its home ports, with vessels of the Russian Black Sea Fleet venturing into the Mediterranean on a frequent basis. Armament consists of six (four on export boats) anti-ship missiles carried in container-launchers alongside the bridge, plus either two 57mm (2.25in) or one 76mm (2.99in) gun and a 30mm (1.18in) cannon. For air defence the Nanuchka class also carries a short-range surface-to-air missile system. This armament fit is considerably more powerful than is common on most missile boats and allows the Nanuchka class to act as offshore patrol vessels. Survivability is enhanced by the possession of credible anti-air weapons.

SPECIFICATIONS

TYPE: *Corvette*

COUNTRY OF ORIGIN: *Soviet Union/Russia*

DISPLACEMENT: *569 tonnes (560 long tons)*

DIMENSIONS: *59.3m (195ft) Beam: 12.6m (41ft) Draught: 2.4m (8ft)*

MACHINERY: *3 x diesel engines; 3 x shafts*

MAXIMUM SPEED: *32 knots (59km/h)*

ARMAMENT: *6 x SS-N-9 anti-ship missiles; 1 x SA-N-4 surface-to-air missile system; 2 x 57mm (2.25in) guns*

LAUNCHED: *1968*

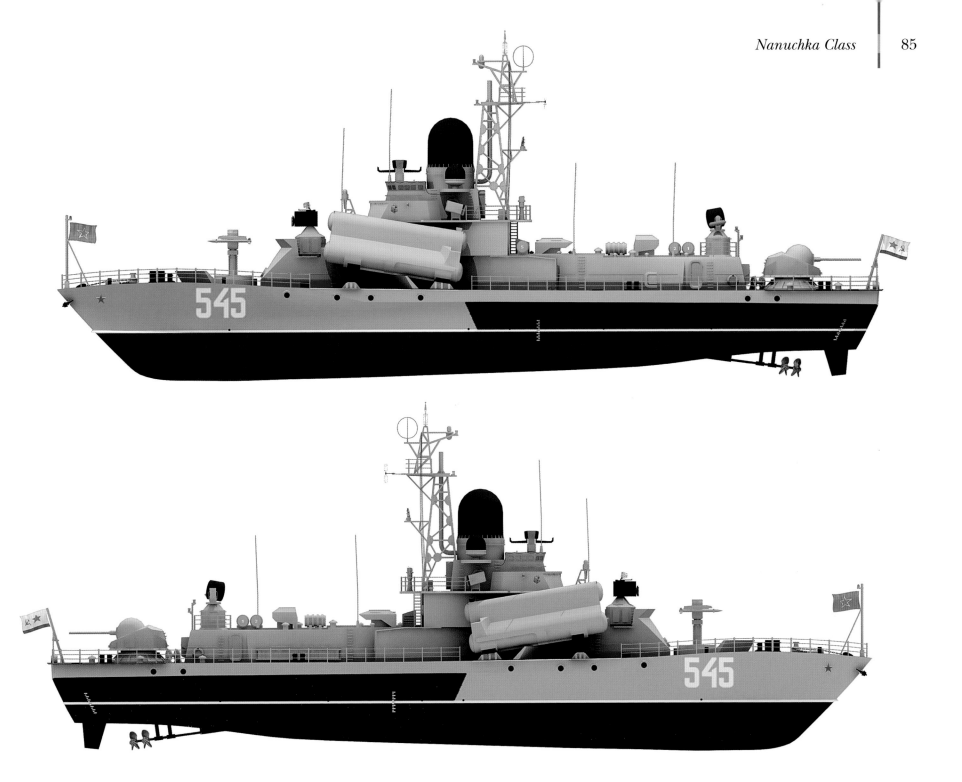

Missile Delivery System

The Nanuchka class can function as a patrol boat, but it is obvious from the size of the missile container-launchers relative to the rest of the vessel that missile delivery is the class's primary mission.

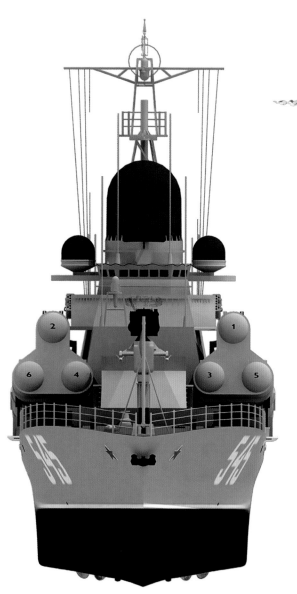

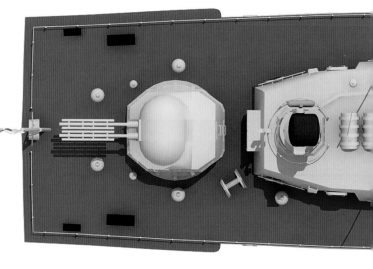

MAIN FEATURES

- Large missile boat with an operating range of 2500 nautical miles

- Missile armament allows anti-ship attacks out to 110 nautical miles

- Engines are reportedly unreliable

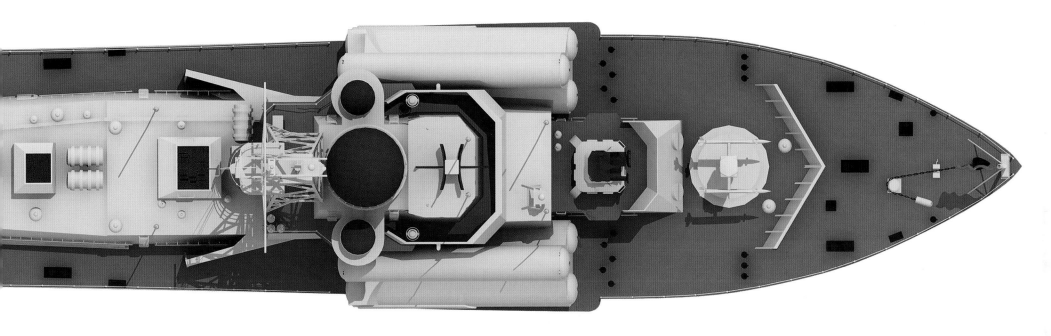

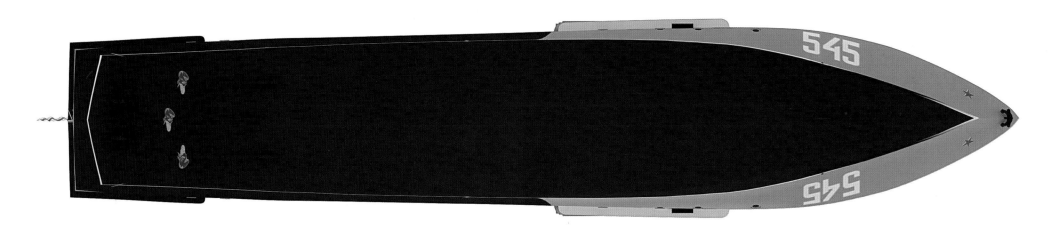

DEFENCE AND ATTACK

Although better defended than most missile boats, Nanuchkas remain essentially expendable missile platforms. Good air defences make it more likely that the vessel will survive long enough to launch its weapons, potentially justifying their expense. Most Nanuchkas of the Russian Navy have been withdrawn from service, and some sold overseas.

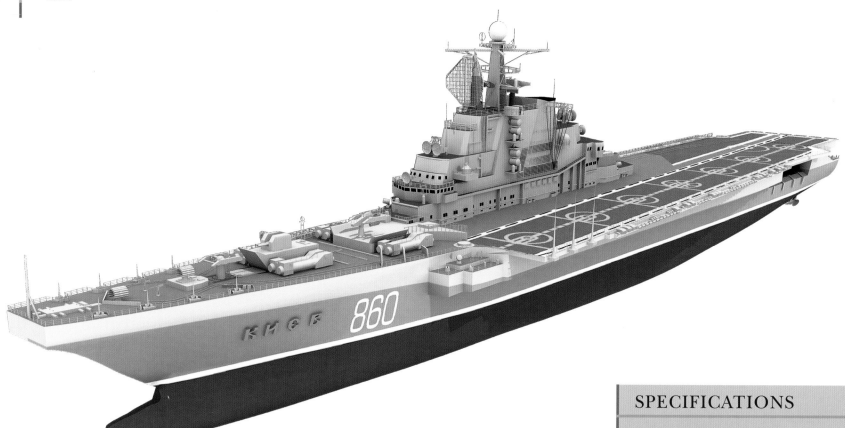

Kiev

The Kiev class was a combination of cruiser and aircraft carrier, termed an 'air-capable ship' in Russian parlance. It was capable of engaging surface, submarine or airborne targets with its own weapons, and carried up to 30 aircraft. Its air group comprised a mix of helicopters and vertical takeoff Yak-38 'Forger' fighters of relatively limited range and capability. The former Soviet Union had never built aircraft carriers before the Kiev class (the vessels served in the Soviet and then Russian navy). The hybrid cruiser/carrier design was chosen in the belief that this was a more cost-effective means of taking aircraft to sea than a full-deck carrier. The short deck made it impossible to operate high-capability aircraft, but even fairly basic fighters can be effective against helicopters and reconnaissance or anti-submarine aircraft.

SPECIFICATIONS

TYPE: *Aircraft carrier*

COUNTRY OF ORIGIN: *Soviet Union/Russia*

DISPLACEMENT: *42,674 tonnes (42,000 long tons)*

DIMENSIONS: *Length: 275m (902ft) Beam: 47.2m (155ft) Draught: 8.2m (27ft)*

MACHINERY: *4 x geared steam turbines; 4 x shafts*

MAXIMUM SPEED: *32 knots (59km/h)*

ARMAMENT: *Aircraft: 12 x Yak-38M; 20 x Kamov Ka-25 or Kamov Ka-27 helicopters. Weapons: 4 x twin SS-N-12 Sandbox SSM launchers; 2 x twin SA-N-3 Shtorm SAM launchers; 2 x twin SA-N-4 Gecko SAM launchers, 2 x twin 76mm (3in) guns, 8 x AK-630 30mm (1.18in) CIWS, 10 x 533mm (21in) torpedo tubes; 1 x twin SUW-N-1 ASW rocket launcher, 2 x RBU-6000 anti-submarine rocket launchers*

LAUNCHED: *1972*

Potent Surface Combatant

The hybrid cruiser/carrier concept was a uniquely Soviet one, and has not been repeated since. The heavy armament of the Kievs made them arguably more potent as surface combatants than as aviation platforms. It has been suggested that the intended role of the Kiev class was the support of amphibious operations, a role that its short-range YAK-38s were entirely capable of carrying out. The class was also capable of carrying out sea denial operations, preventing hostile forces from entering important sea areas, such as those used by the Russian ballistic missile submarine fleet.

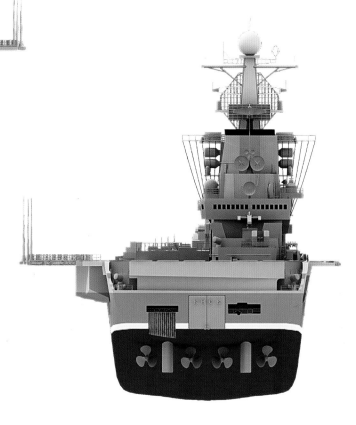

MAIN FEATURES

- Unique hybrid cruiser/carrier design
- Armed with long-range anti-ship missiles in addition to aircraft-carried weapons
- No catapult or 'ski jump' for high-speed aircraft launch

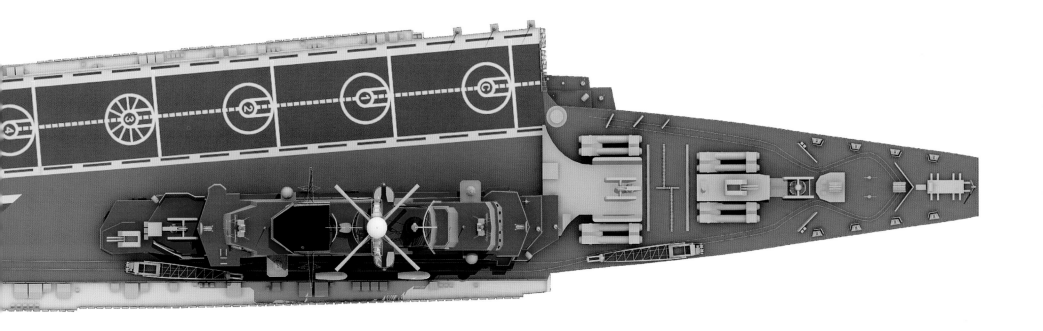

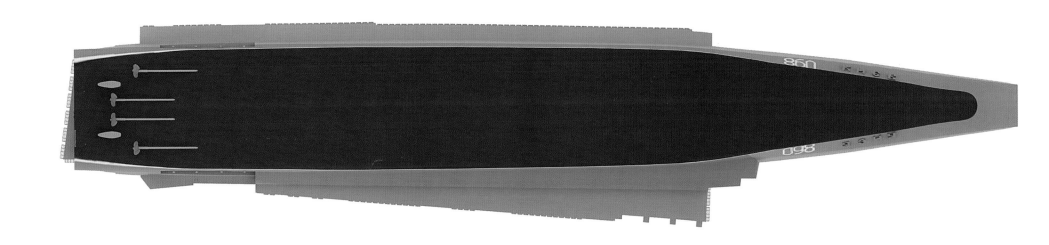

LIMITED SERVICEABILITY

Four vessels of the Kiev class were built, entering service in 1975. Examples served with the Northern Fleet, the Black Sea Fleet and the Pacific Fleet. By 1991, however, the existing Yak-38 force was unserviceable, and no replacement aircraft existed. Three members of the class were scrapped; one was sold to India and is being modified to operate MiG-29K and Sea Harrier aircraft. The most obvious alteration will be the addition of a 'ski-jump' at the fore end of the launch deck.

SPECIFICATIONS

TYPE: *Destroyer*

COUNTRY OF ORIGIN: *United States of America*

DISPLACEMENT: *8169 tonnes (8040 long tons)*

DIMENSIONS: *172m (564ft) Beam: 16.8m (55ft) Draught: 8.8m (29ft)*

MACHINERY: *4 x General Electric LM2500 gas turbines; 2 x shafts*

MAXIMUM SPEED: *32.5 knots (60km/h)*

ARMAMENT: *Aircraft: 2 x Sikorsky SH-60 Seahawk LAMPS III helicopters. Weapons: 2 x 127 mm (5in) 54 cal. Mark 45 guns; 2 x 20mm (0.78in) Phalanx CIWS Mark 15 guns; 1 x 8-cell NATO Sea Sparrow Mark 29 missile launcher; 2 x quad AGM-84 Harpoon missile launchers; 2 x Mark 32 triple 324mm (12.75in) torpedo tubes (Mk 46 torpedoes); 1 x 61-cell Mk 41 VLS launcher for Tomahawk missiles*

LAUNCHED: *1943*

Spruance

The Spruance class of destroyers were the first US Navy ships to be powered by gas turbine engines. Their primary role was anti-submarine warfare, particularly the defence of carrier battle groups against the new generation of submarines emerging during the late 1970s and early 1980s. As initially built, the Spruance class was very lightly armed despite the vessels' large size. Primary armament was anti-submarine weapons: Mark 46 torpedoes and weapons carried by the vessel's two small helicopters. An ASROC launcher was initially fitted, but was later removed. This created an effective anti-submarine platform, but the class carried only guns for surface action and a short-range SAM system for air defence.

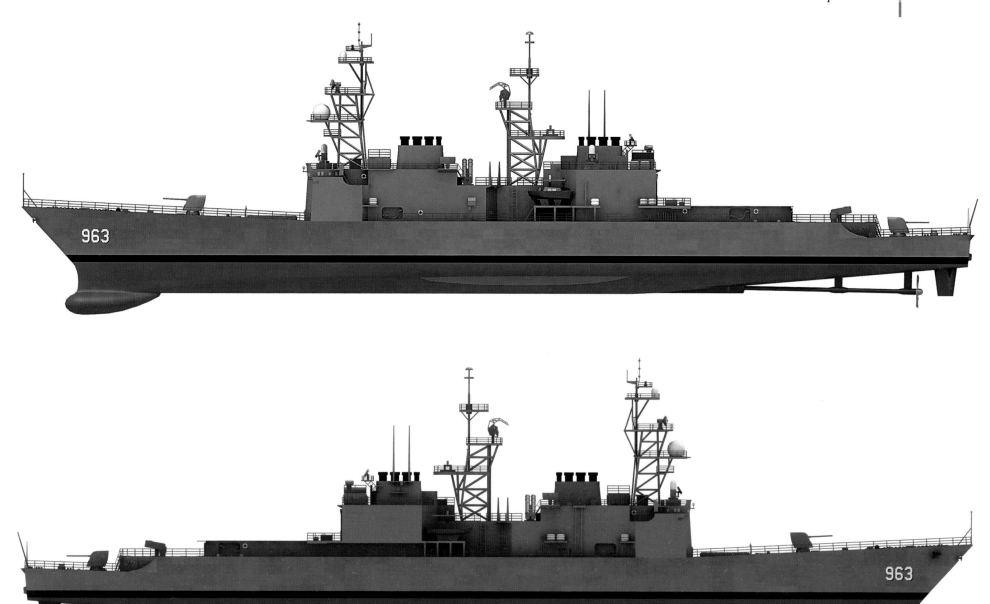

Multirole Platform

As initially built, the Spruance class attracted criticism with regard to its light armament. The class later matured into an effective multirole platform, receiving better air defences and greatly increased surface warfare capability. Lightweight Kevlar armour was also added, increasing an already large displacement, but it remained an expensive alternative to vessels designed from the outset to serve in this role.

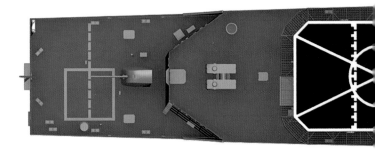

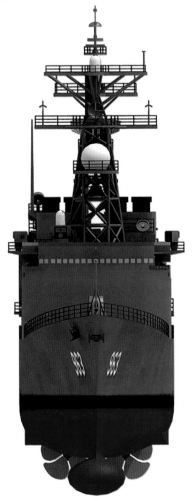

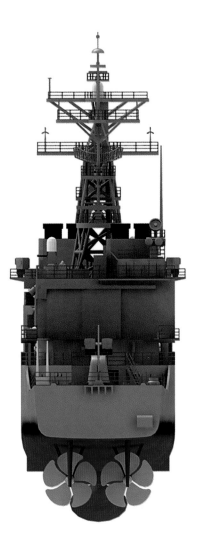

MAIN FEATURES

- Large multi-role destroyer
- Excellent anti-submarine platform
- First US Navy gas turbine-powered ship

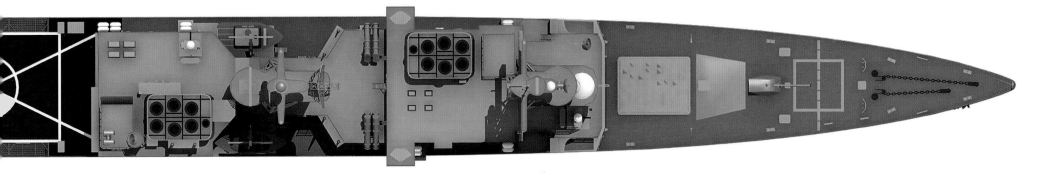

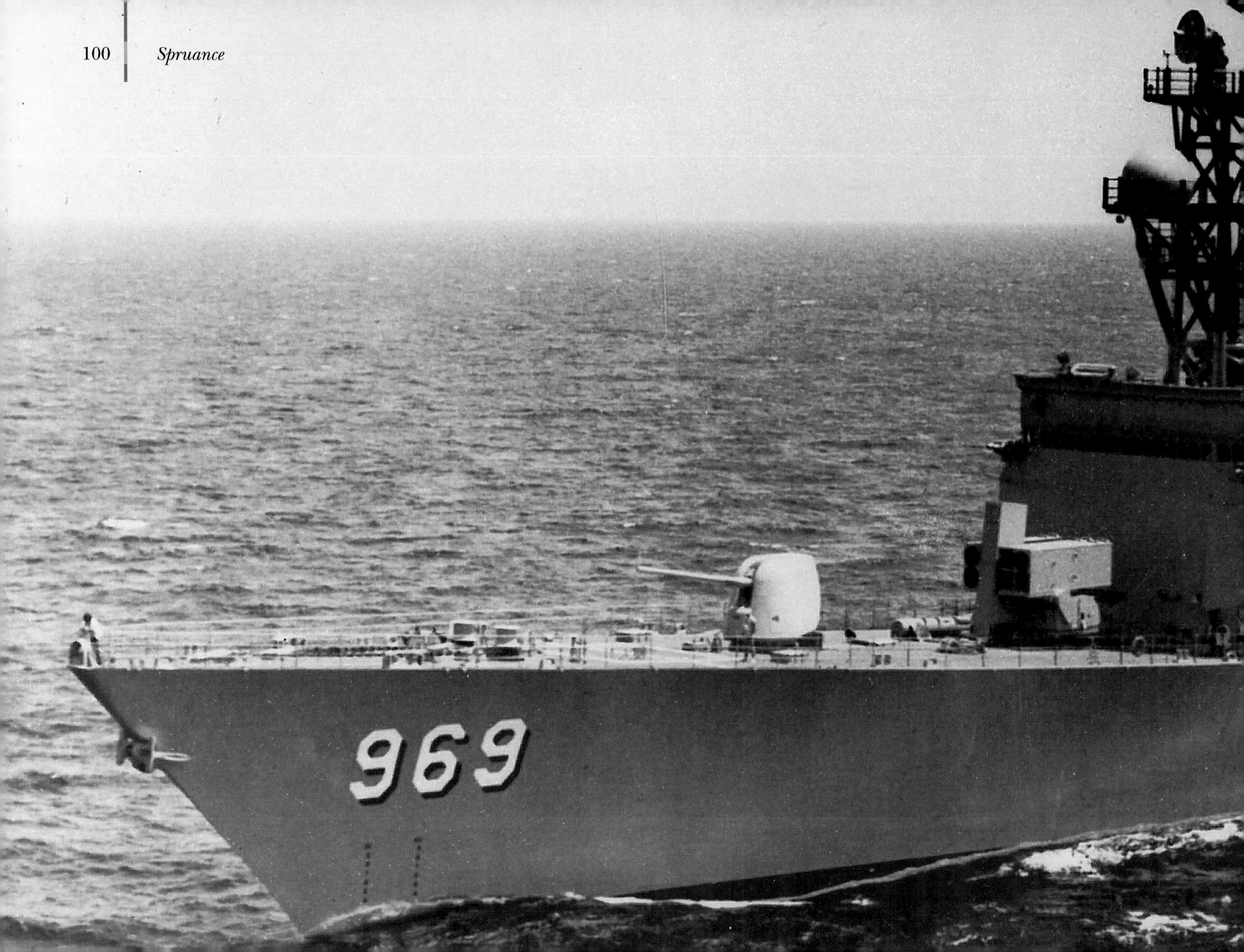
969

SPECIALIZED DUTIES

The Spruance class was intended to serve as part of a task force, providing top-end anti-submarine defence for high-value targets such as a carrier battle group. In this role its deficiencies in anti-surface armament were likely to be covered by aircraft or other vessels. As an initially very specialized ship, the class had high running costs and was not deemed cost-effective to conduct a service life extending upgrade. The class was decommissioned in the mid-2000s, with USS Spruance herself paying off in 2005.

Tarawa

USS *Tarawa* is the lead ship of her class. Although her general shape and ability to operate fixed-wing aircraft lead some observers to mistake *Tarawa* for an aircraft carrier, she is in fact an amphibious warfare platform with the capability to operate aircraft. Her primary role is at the centre of an Amphibious Readiness Group capable of landing US Marines ashore and assisting them with air strikes and logistical support. *Tarawa* can act as a flagship for a senior naval or land forces commander and has extensive medical facilities equipped to the standard of a major hospital. She is armed with light gun and missile systems for defence against air and missile threats, but would usually rely on her escorts, or perhaps Marine Corps aircraft, to deal with enemy vessels.

SPECIFICATIONS

TYPE: *Amphibious assault ship*

COUNTRY OF ORIGIN: *United States of America*

DISPLACEMENT: *39,524 tonnes (38,900 long tons)*

DIMENSIONS: *250m (820ft) Beam: 32m (105ft) Draught: 7.9m (26ft)*

MACHINERY: *Two boilers, two geared steam turbines*

MAXIMUM SPEED: *24 knots (44km/h)*

ARMAMENT: *Aircraft: Up to 35 helicopters and 8 x AV-8B Harrier II VSTOL aircraft. Weapons: 4 x Mk 38 Mod 1 25mm (0.98in) Bushmaster cannons; 5 x M2HB 50 cal. machine guns; 2 x Mk 15 Phalanx CIWS; 2 x Mk 49 RAM launchers*

LAUNCHED: *1943*

Specialized Mission

Landing ships with a flight deck are often mistaken for aircraft carriers, but their mission is more specialized. The most obvious difference is the absence of an angled landing deck; landing ships do not operate high-performance aircraft that need specialist recovery systems. USS Tarawa's *primary capabilities rest with an entire battalion of Marine Corps personnel, supported by an air group of more than 30 helicopters, plus eight AV-8B Harrier jets.*

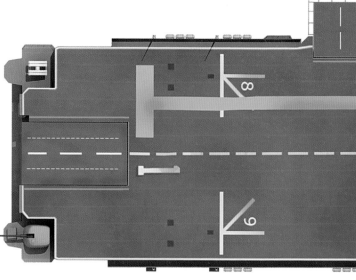

MAIN FEATURES

- Large air-capable amphibious warfare platform
- Light air and missile defence armament
- Stern well-deck accommodates landing craft

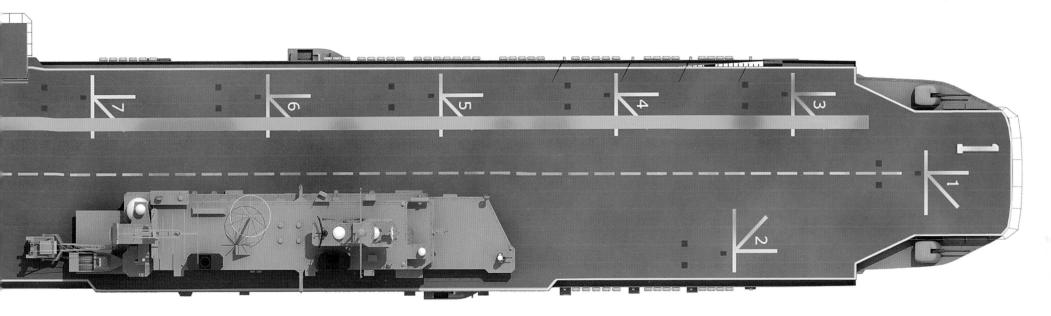

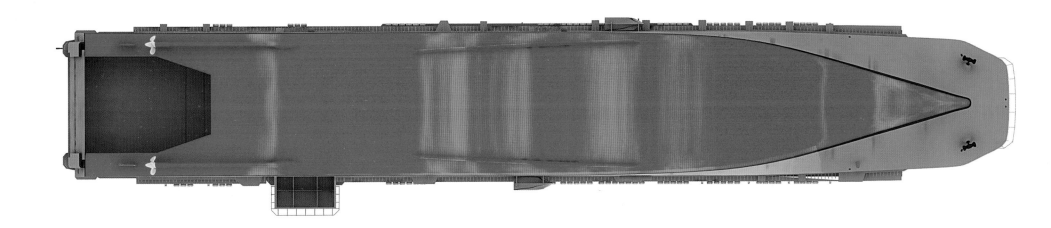

TACTICAL INTEGRITY

The Tarawa class is designed to maintain the 'tactical integrity' of its US Marine formations, putting a balanced force ashore with all elements in the right place at the right time. USS Tarawa, *for instance, has undertaken several operational deployments, during which she has supported peacekeepers, rescued distressed mariners and provided humanitarian assistance. During the 1991 Gulf War she took part in a feint, moving as if to land Marines on the Iraqi coastline, to deceive the enemy as to Coalition intentions. Her aircraft later helped to enforce the no-fly zones over Iraq. She helped to protect the crippled USS* Cole *in 2000, and has also taken part in operations in Afghanistan.*

Stephen W. Groves

USS *Stephen W. Groves* is an Oliver Hazard Perry class frigate, a general-purpose warship whose primary role is anti-submarine warfare and the escort of high-value assets such as amphibious assault ships, replenishment vessels and aircraft carriers. She also serves as a training ship for naval reservists. The O.H. Perry class was designed in the mid-1970w as a low-cost warship to replace the large numbers of World War II–era vessels that were due for retirement. 'Block obsolescence' of this sort presented the US Navy with substantial budgetary problems. Even with midlife upgrades, significant numbers of ships had come to the end of their careers, but the US Navy needed a certain number of hulls to cover its responsibilities. The solution was to design and build an inexpensive vessel of modest capabilities, saving money for a small number of top-end combatants.

SPECIFICATIONS

TYPE: *Guided-missile frigate*

COUNTRY OF ORIGIN: *United States of America*

DISPLACEMENT: *4200 tonnes (4134 long tons)*

DIMENSIONS: *Length: 138m (453ft) Beam: 14m (46ft) Draught: 6.7m (22ft)*

MACHINERY: *2 x General Electric LM2500-30 gas turbines; 2 x Auxiliary Propulsion Units*

MAXIMUM SPEED: *29 knots (54km/h)*

ARMAMENT: *Aircraft: 2 x SH-60 helicopters. Weapons: 1 x OTO Melara Mk 75 76mm/62 cal. gun; 2 x Mk 32 triple-tube 324mm (12.75in) launchers for Mk 46 torpedoes; 1 x Vulcan Phalanx CIWS; 4 x 50 cal. (12.7mm) machine guns; 1 x Mk 13 Mod 4 single-arm launcher for AGM-84 Harpoon anti-ship missiles and SM-1MR Standard anti-ship/air missiles*

LAUNCHED: *1981*

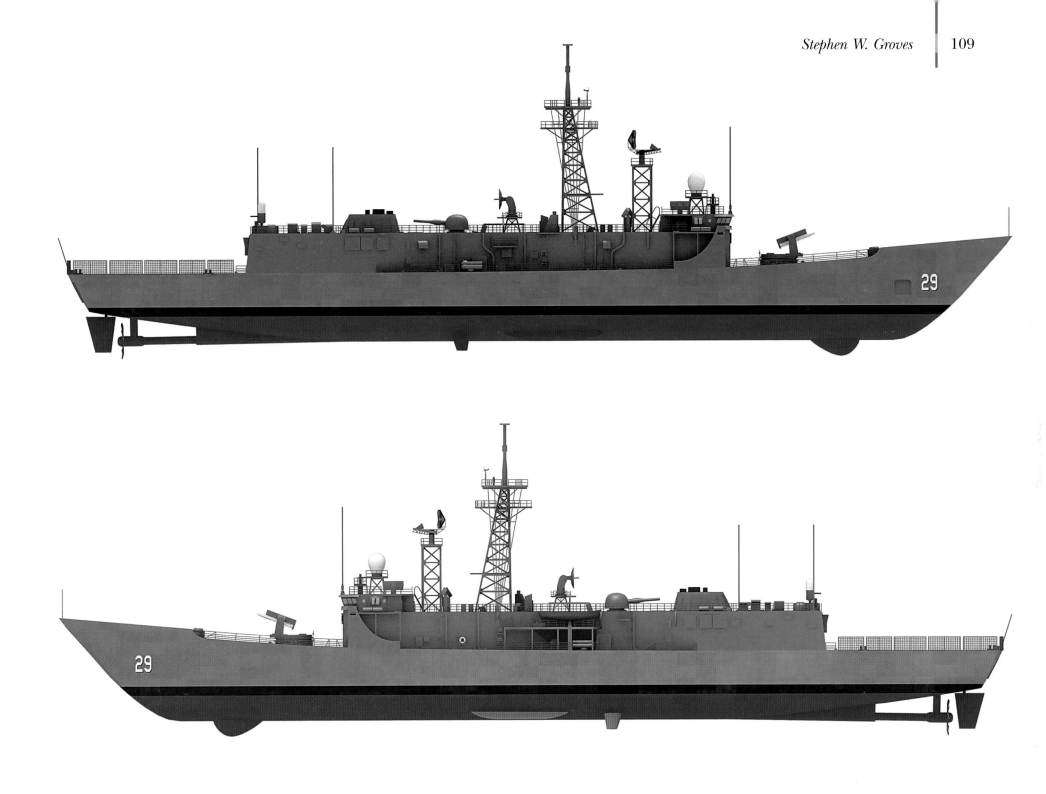

Practical Escorts

Many naval missions do not require a hugely capable vessel, but can be carried out by inexpensive ships such as the Perry class. In a major war, these vessels can still contribute to a task force as escorts and additional sensor platforms.

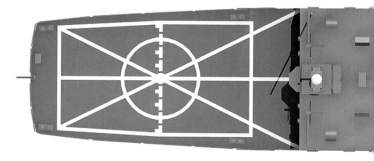

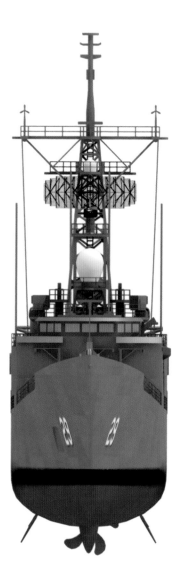

MAIN FEATURES

- General-purpose patrol and escort frigate
- Light gun armament and anti-submarine torpedoes
- Retractable auxiliary propulsion pods for docking and other manoeuvres

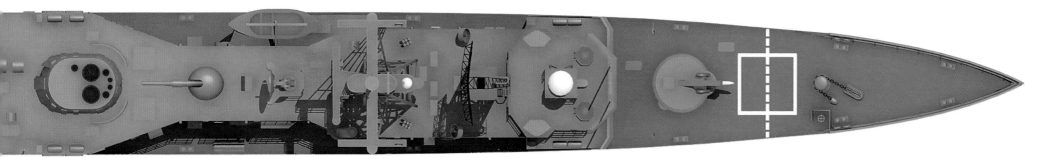

SECURITY OPERATIONS

Commissioned in 1982 as a general-purpose frigate,
Stephen W. Groves *is now deployed in a security role. Since
the removal of her missile armament, she has transferred
to the patrol and enforcement role, undertaking operations
against fast drug-smuggling boats and intercepting vessels
suspected of carrying narcotics. This does not require warfighting capability, but presents an entirely different set of
challenges to a warship and her crew. In this role the ship's
light weapons and helicopters are her main assets.*

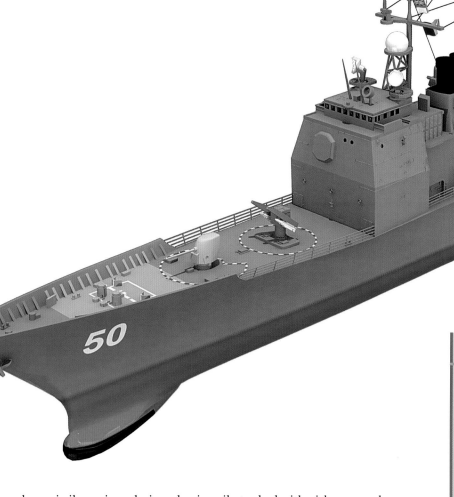

Valley Forge

USS *Valley Forge* was a Ticonderoga class missile cruiser, designed primarily to deal with airborne and missile threats. She was one of the first vessels to carry the Aegis integrated air defence system, and the first to be decommissioned. The Aegis system uses flat phased array radar panels, rather than rotating antennae, and can track more than 100 targets at once. *Valley Forge*'s primary armament was her surface-to-air missiles, backed up by two medium-calibre guns, Harpoon anti-ship missiles and anti-submarine torpedoes. Close-in weapon systems and heavy machine guns were also carried for short-range defence, along with two light helicopters for anti-submarine and utility work. Some vessels of the Ticonderoga class have been decommissioned, including *Valley Forge*. Others have acquired new capabilities, including the ability to intercept ballistic missiles and even satellites.

SPECIFICATIONS

TYPE: *Cruiser*

COUNTRY OF ORIGIN: *United States of America*

DISPLACEMENT: *9750 tonnes (9596 long tons)*

DIMENSIONS: *Length: 173m (568ft) Beam: 16.8m (55ft) Draught: 10.2m (33ft)*

MACHINERY: *4 x General Electric LM2500 gas turbines*

MAXIMUM SPEED: *32.5 knots (60km/h)*

ARMAMENT: *Aircraft: 2 x Sikorsky SH-60 Seahawk LAMPS III helicopters. Weapons: 2 x Mk 26 missile launchers; 88 x RIM-66 SM-2 surface-to-air missiles; 8 x RGM-84 Harpoon missiles; 2 x Mk 45 127mm (5in)/54 cal. lightweight gun; 4 x 12.7 mm (0.5in) 50 cal. guns; 2 x Phalanx CIWS; 2 x Mk 32 324mm (12.75in) triple torpedo tubes*

LAUNCHED: *1984*

Missile Launch Systems

Vertical launch systems permit most of the missiles aboard the Ticonderoga class to be carried below decks, where they are better protected from enemy action and the effects of the nautical environment. The first five ships of the class, however, carried conventional twin missile launchers fore and aft.

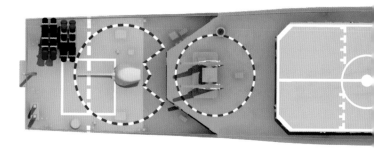

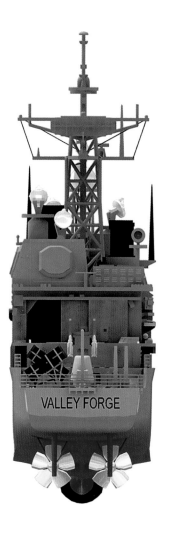

MAIN FEATURES

- Large anti-aircraft cruiser
- Missile armament directed by advanced phased array radar system
- Decommissioned and sunk as a target in 2004

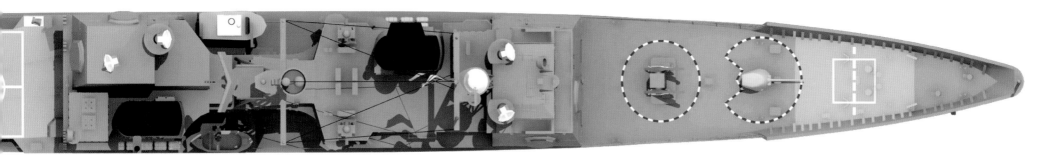

ESCORT AND PROTECT

USS Valley Forge*'s career included escorting tankers through the troubled Persian Gulf during the Iran–Iraq war, and a deployment to the same region during the 1991 Gulf War. She later deployed as part of the naval force protecting humanitarian aid efforts off east Africa and undertook patrol work as part of international drug-traffic enforcement efforts. After taking part in joint US-Russian naval exercises in 1995,* Valley Forge *was again deployed in the Persian Gulf. She later returned to the drug enforcement role, before being decommissioned in 2004 after 20 years in service.*

Sea Shadow

Sea Shadow is an experimental vessel developed as a testbed for new 'stealth' technologies. Often referred to as 'USS *Sea Shadow*', this vessel has never been commissioned into the US Navy, making the designation a misnomer. It is, however, closely associated with the navy and is listed among the navy's miscellaneous craft. *Sea Shadow* is based on a Small Waterplane Area Twin Hull (SWATH) design, with torpedo-shaped hulls located underwater. These provide stability while ensuring as little drag as possible. Propellers at the aft end of the underwater hulls provide propulsion at up to 28 knots. The vessel is steered and kept stable by canards and stabilizing fins on the underwater hulls. *Sea Shadow* is not a warship, but a development platform for new concepts and technologies. Data gathered using her has been used in the development of advanced warships such as the Zumwalt Class, making these projects less financially risky.

SPECIFICATIONS

Type: *Experimental stealth ship*

Country of Origin: *United States of America*

Displacement: *572 tonnes (563 long tons)*

Dimensions: *Length: 50m (164ft) Beam: 21m (69ft) Draught: 4.6m (15ft)*

Machinery: *2 x Detroit Diesel 12V-149TI engines, 2 x shafts*

Maximum Speed: *28 knots (52km/h)*

Armament: *None*

Launched: *1985*

Unique Systems

The underwater component of Sea Shadow's *hull is torpedo-shaped and is of sufficient displacement to allow the main hull to remain well clear of the water. Rather than rudders, the vessel is steered using fins on the inboard sides of the lower hulls. Her hull, propulsion and manoeuvring systems have all been used as development tools for systems incorporated into other vessels. The stabilizer/canard system is now used aboard some oceanographic ships, while the hull form has influenced a new generation of stealthy warships.*

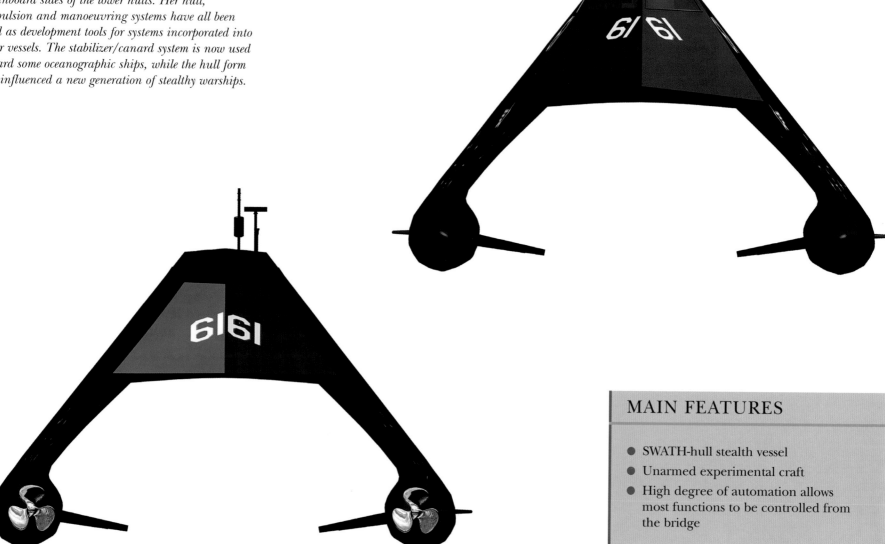

MAIN FEATURES

- SWATH-hull stealth vessel
- Unarmed experimental craft
- High degree of automation allows most functions to be controlled from the bridge

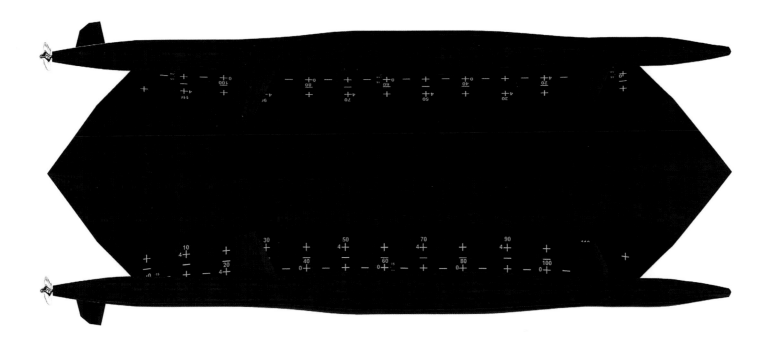

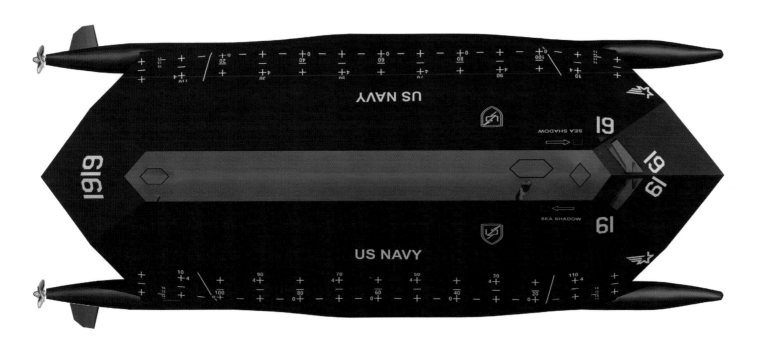

ADVANCED TESTBED

Sea Shadow began its career in 1985, initially in great
secrecy. It has at times been laid up and even listed for
disposal, although new experimental programmes may result
in renewed interest in an advanced testbed where new
concepts can be trialled without drawing on frontline combat
units for resources.

Norfolk

HMS *Norfolk* was the lead ship of the Type 23 ('Iron Duke') class of frigates in Royal Navy service. Like many frigates the Type 23 was designed primarily for anti-submarine warfare, but grew into a multirole design equipped for surface action as well as air defence. Vessels of this class are still in service with the Royal Navy, although *Norfolk* now serves in the Chilean navy as *Almirante Cochrane*. Anti-submarine armament consists of four torpedo tubes and a helicopter equipped with ASW weapons. *Norfolk* has a bow-mounted sonar and a towed sonar array for the sub-hunting role. She is also equipped with eight Harpoon anti-ship missiles and a vertical-launch system for Seawolf anti-air missiles. A general-purpose 114mm (4.5in) gun is shipped, along with two 30mm (1.18in) cannon for close-in air defence. These weapons can also be used against surface targets.

SPECIFICATIONS

TYPE: *Frigate*

COUNTRY OF ORIGIN: *United Kingdom*

DISPLACEMENT: *4900 tonnes (4823 long tons)*

DIMENSIONS: *Length: 133m (436ft) Beam: 16.1m (53ft) Draught: 5.5m (18ft)*

MACHINERY: *2 x Rolls-Royce Spey SM1A gas turbines; 4 x Paxman Valenta diesel engines; 2 x GEC electric motors*

MAXIMUM SPEED: *28 knots (52km/h)*

ARMAMENT: *2 x quad AGM-84 Harpoon launchers; 32 x Vertical Launch Sea Wolf Missile System; 1 x 114mm (4.5in) Mk.8 Mod 1 gun; 2 x Oerlikon 30mm (1.18in) cannon; 4 x Sting Ray Torpedo System*

LAUNCHED: *1987*

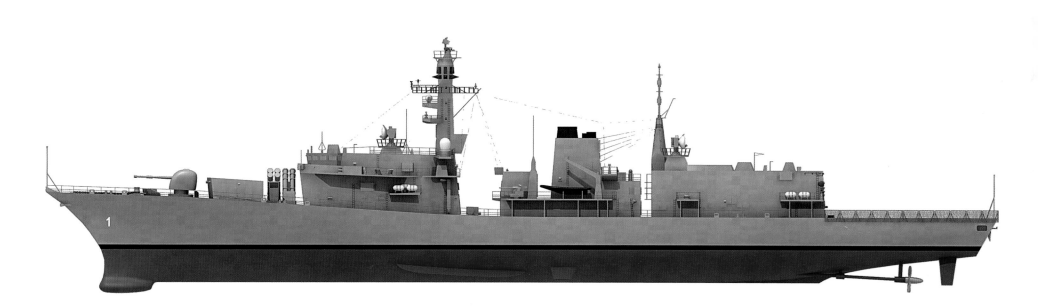

Vertical Launch

Vertical launch systems require considerably less deck space than conventional missile systems, and can often be upgraded to carry different missiles without undue difficulty. HMS Norfolk *was the first vessel to receive the vertically launched Seawolf and the new 114mm (4.5in) Mod 1 gun. She is seen in these images in Chilean navy service as* Almirante Cochrane.

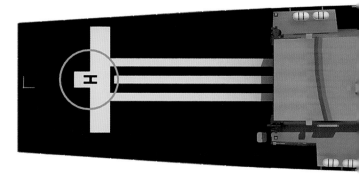

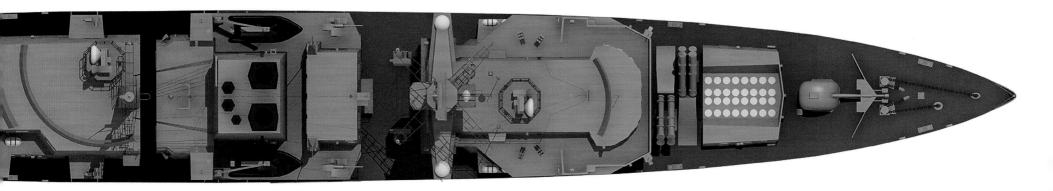

GAS TURBINE POWER

Running on her diesel engines, HMS Norfolk *could cruise at an economical speed of 15 knots. Her gas turbines enabled her to reach 28 knots, albeit at the cost of increased fuel consumption and self-noise that greatly reduced sonar effectiveness. HMS* Norfolk *was the first Royal Navy warship to visit South Africa for many years, and has served in the North and South Atlantic, as well as the Caribbean, the Mediterranean and the Persian Gulf. In 2005 HMS* Norfolk *was decommissioned, and was sold to Chile along with two of her sister ships. She remains in service.*

Karel Doorman

Guided missile frigates designed and built for the Netherlands navy, the Karel Doorman class is derived from the larger Kortenaer (or 'Standard') frigates and were primarily conceived as patrol ships. A platoon of marines can be carried, along with inflatable boats for their use. In wartime these ships would assist more capable vessels as escorts, mainly in the anti-submarine role. Armament consists of Harpoon anti-ship missiles and a 76mm (3in) gun for surface combat, plus anti-aircraft missiles and a close-in weapon system for missile defence. Antisubmarine armament consists of torpedo tubes and helicopter-carried weapons. Two 20mm (0.78in) cannon are also shipped. These weapons have some anti-aircraft capability, but are primarily useful when conducting stop-and-search operations such as in the drug enforcement role.

SPECIFICATIONS

TYPE: *Frigate*

COUNTRY OF ORIGIN: *Netherlands*

DISPLACEMENT: *2800 tonnes (2756 long tons)*

DIMENSIONS: *Length: 122.3m (401ft) Beam: 14.4m (47ft) Draught: 6.2m (20ft)*

MACHINERY: *2 x Rolls Royce Spey 1A gas turbines; 2 x Stork-Werkspoor diesel engines*

MAXIMUM SPEED: *30 knots (56km/h)*

ARMAMENT: *1 x Oto Melara 76mm (3in) anti-air/anti-surface gun; 1 x Oerlikon 20mm (0.78in) light cannon; 1 x Sea Sparrow Missile Vertical Launch System (VLS); 8 x RGM-84 Harpoon missiles; 1 x Goalkeeper CIWS; Mk. 46 torpedoes*

LAUNCHED: *1988*

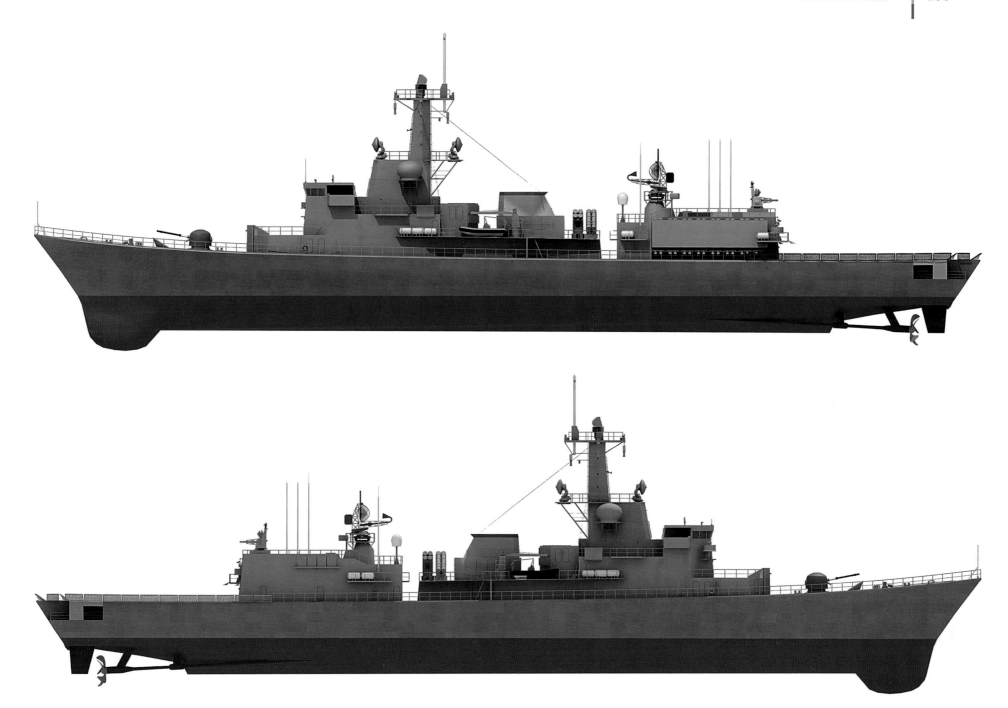

Efficient Crews

Crew training costs and salaries represent a significant portion of naval expenditure. Small, highly automated vessels such as members of the Karel Doorman class are attractive because of their relatively low crew costs.

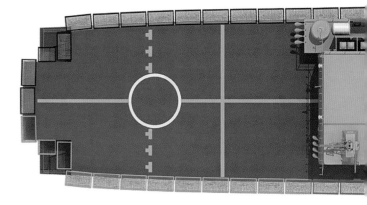

MAIN FEATURES

- Small, inexpensive patrol frigate
- Capable of engaging surface, air and submarine threats
- Extensive automation reduces crew size and thus operating costs

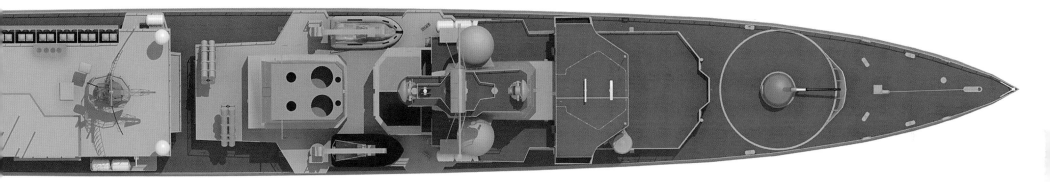

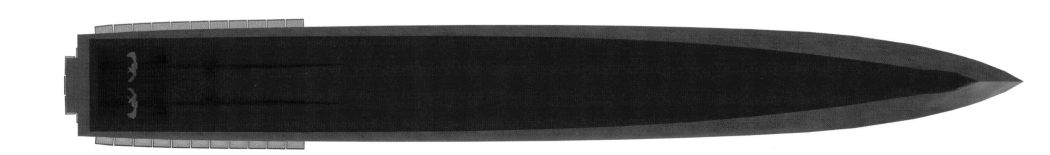

SWITCH IN SERVICE

The name ship of the class, HNLMS Karel Doorman, *was sold to Belgium in 2005 and now serves with the Belgian navy. In Netherlands service she served in the patrol role, enforcing international drugs laws in the Caribbean, and was deployed as part of UN forces off the coast of the former Yugoslavia. Since transferring to the Belgian navy, the vessel has been renamed F930* Leopold I. *She began her career with a deployment to East Africa. Others of the class have been sold to Portugal.*

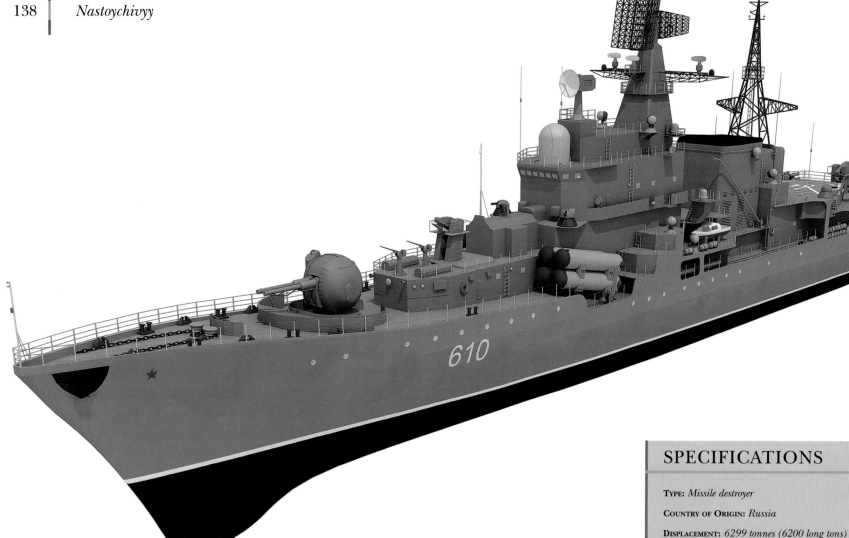

Nastoychivyy

The Sovremenny class of destroyers, of which the *Nastoychivyy* is a member, was designed in the 1970s and was developed from a vessel intended to support amphibious operations. The class is optimized for surface action, although it carries heavy anti-air defences. Russian vessels of the Cold War era were expected to have to operate under the heavy air threat posed by US carrier forces. Armament is based on long-range surface-to-surface missiles backed up by 130mm (5.11in) guns. Surface-to-air missiles and two close-in weapon systems provide air defence, and there are both torpedoes and an anti-submarine rocket launcher for ASW work. A single helicopter is also carried.

SPECIFICATIONS

TYPE: *Missile destroyer*

COUNTRY OF ORIGIN: *Russia*

DISPLACEMENT: *6299 tonnes (6200 long tons)*

DIMENSIONS: *Length: 156m (512ft) Beam: 17.3m (57ft) Draught: 6.5m (21ft)*

MACHINERY: *2 shaft steam turbines, 4 boilers*

MAXIMUM SPEED: *32 knots (59km/h)*

ARMAMENT: *Aircraft: 1 x Ka-27 'Helix' helicopter. Weapons: 2 x 4 SS-N-22 'Sunburn' Moskit SSM; 2 x SA-N-7 'Gadfly' SAM; 4 x 130mm (5.11in) guns; 4 x 30mm (0.78in) AK-630 Gatling guns; 4 x 553mm (21in) torpedo tubes; 2 x RBU-1000 ASW rockets*

LAUNCHED: *1991*

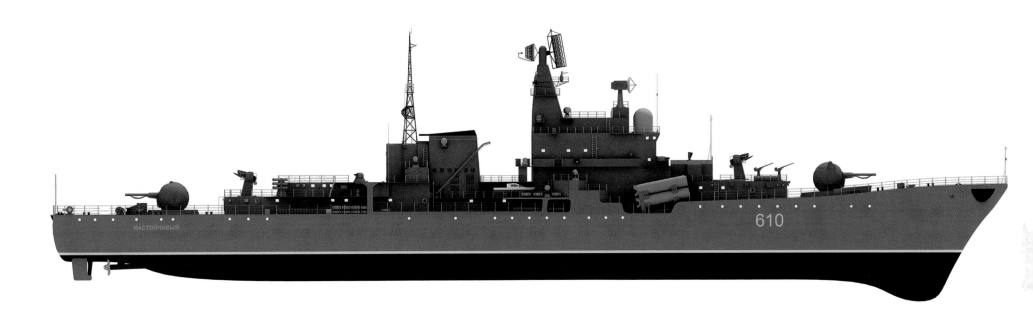

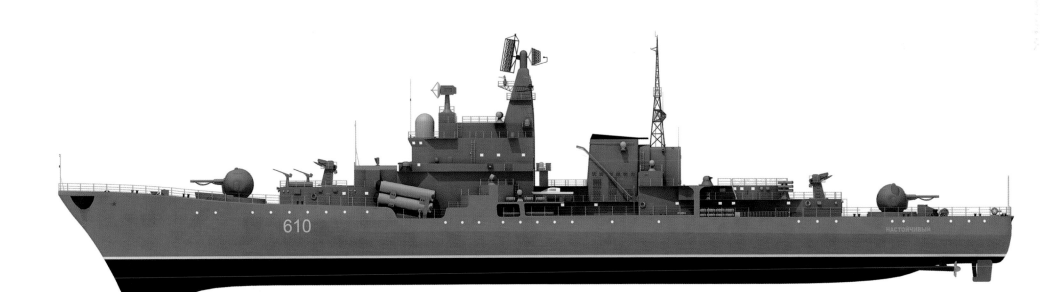

Nuclear Capability

The Sovremenny class is large for a destroyer type; some authorities term them cruisers instead. Eighteen were built for the former Soviet and now Russian navy, of which five remain in service. The main missile battery can launch either conventional or nuclear warheads. The latter were primarily envisaged as useful against high-value targets such as a US carrier group during an all-out war. The use of nuclear weapons at sea, rather than land use, was thought to be less likely to lead to nuclear escalation.

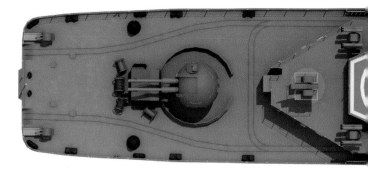

MAIN FEATURES

- Multirole destroyer geared mainly towards surface action
- Long-range missile armament
- Export versions available with altered equipment

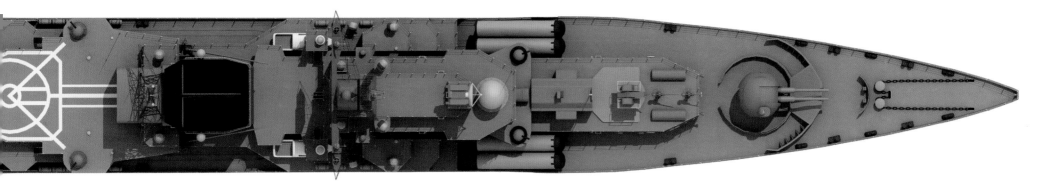

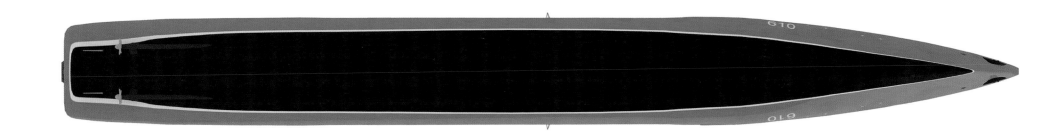

AN AGEING CLASS

China bought two modified Sovremenny class destroyers and could potentially build more under licence or alernatively buy them. This class is showing its age, however, and replacement by a more advanced vessel is likely.

Kongo

The Kongo class consists of large destroyers serving with the Japanese Maritime Self-Defence Force and is based on the US Arleigh Burke class of destroyers. Members of the Kongo class are very large, almost in the cruiser range, and have a deep draught. These vessels are intended primarily for 'blue-water' operations and would be limited in the shallow-water littoral environment. The Kongo class is armed with Harpoon anti-ship missiles and a 127mm (5in) gun for surface combat, plus anti-submarine weapons and air defence missiles. Two 20mm (0.78in) Phalanx close-in weapon systems provide last-ditch air or missile defence. The Kongo class has a landing platform for a helicopter, but does not carry or operate one, and cannot provide support to a visiting helicopter.

SPECIFICATIONS

TYPE: *Destroyer*

COUNTRY OF ORIGIN: *Japan*

DISPLACEMENT: *7620 tonnes (7500 long tons)*

DIMENSIONS: *Length: 161m (528ft) Beam: 21m (69ft) Draught: 6.2m (20ft)*

MACHINERY: *4 x Ishikawajima Harima/General Electric LM2500-30 gas turbines; two shafts*

MAXIMUM SPEED: *30 knots (56km/h)*

ARMAMENT: *RGM-84 Harpoon SSM system; SM-2MR Standard SAMs; RUM-139 Vertical Launch ASROC; 1 x 127mm (5in)/54 cal. Oto-Breda Compact Gun; 2 x 20mm (0.78in) Phalanx CIWS; 2 x Type 68 triple torpedo tubes (6 x Mk-46 or Type 73 torpedoes)*

LAUNCHED: *1991*

Flagship for a Squadron
DDG-173 Kongo, *the name ship of a four-vessel class, is equipped to function as flagship for a squadron, which would probably be composed of vessels belonging to other classes. While derived from the US Arleigh Burke class, the Kongo class has a different role and hence significant differences in equipment and layout.*

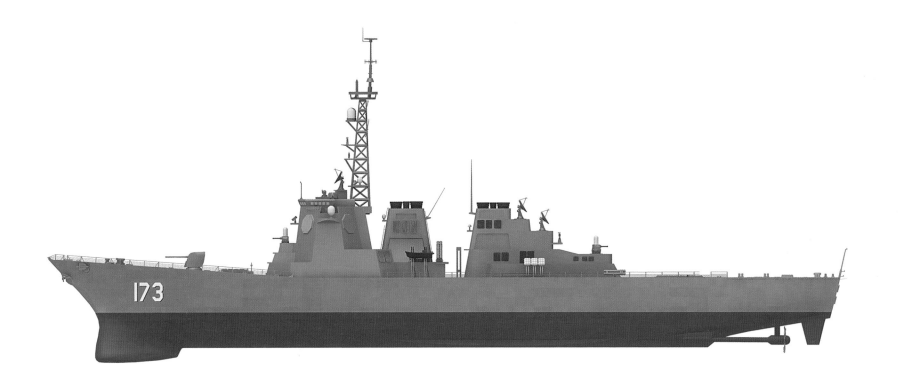

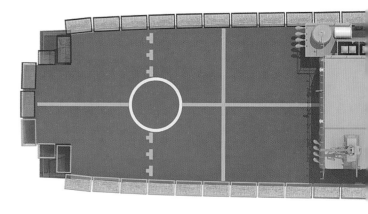

MAIN FEATURES

- Large destroyer capable of engaging a range of threats
- Armament primarily made up of air defence and anti-ship missiles
- Phased-array antennae for AEGIS radar system on superstructure

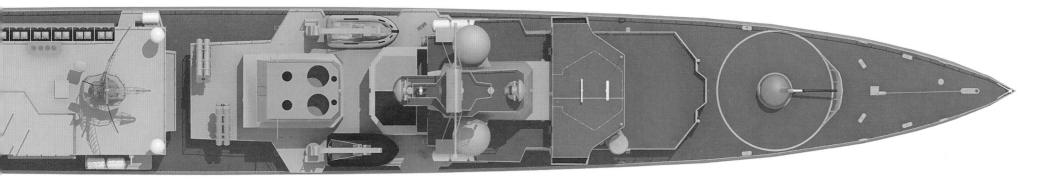

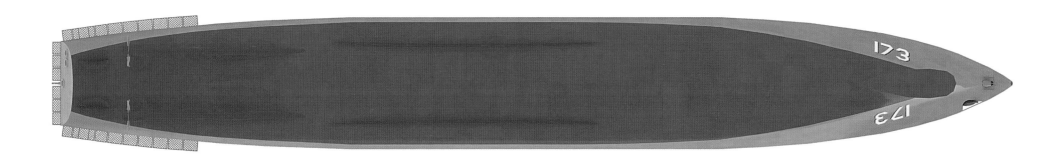

Kongo 149

MOBILE TRACKING

The Japanese Maritime Self-Defence Force is defensive in nature, and lacks the ability to project power over long distances. Thus the four ships of the Kongo class, although derived from the US Arleigh Burke class, do not carry the long-range cruise missiles shipped by those vessels. Concerns over North Korean possession of long-range missiles prompted a conversion programme, enabling the Kongo class to provide theatre ballistic missile defence capability. This permits the vessels to act as mobile tracking platforms, engaging ballistic missiles aimed at the homeland with a modified air defence missile while the threat is still far from its target.

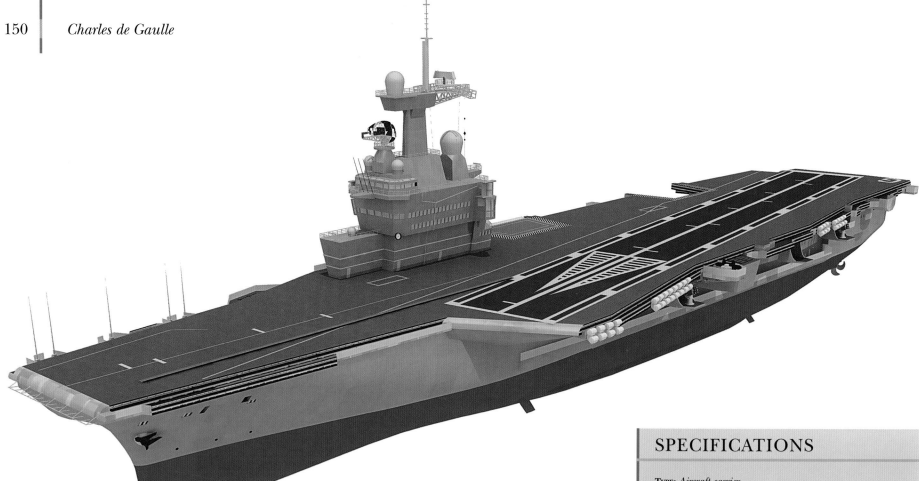

Charles de Gaulle

Charles de Gaulle is the only nuclear-powered aircraft carrier that does not belong to the United States Navy. She is in current service, after a long development and construction period that involved many delays and setbacks. Among other problems, defective propellers limited her speed until suitable replacements could be fabricated. Her air group consists of mulitrole Rafale fighters supported by airborne early warning aircraft and helicopters. She can also carry a force of up to 800 commandos and could swap part of her air group for assault helicopters if necessary. Like all aircraft carriers, *Charles de Gaulle* is lightly armed for self-defence against air threats. Having finally overcome her teething troubles, she has successfully projected French air power over Afghanistan and other troubled regions, playing a significant role in the war against the Taliban.

SPECIFICATIONS

TYPE: *Aircraft carrier*

COUNTRY OF ORIGIN: *France*

DISPLACEMENT: *38,000 tonnes (37,400 long tons)*

DIMENSIONS: *Length: 261.5m (858ft) Beam: 64.4m (211ft) Draught: 9.43m (31ft)*

MACHINERY: *2 x K15 pressurised water reactors; 4 x diesel-electric engines; 2 x shafts*

MAXIMUM SPEED: *27 knots (50km/h)*

ARMAMENT: *Aircraft: 35–40 aircraft, including Rafale, Super Étendard, E-2C Hawkeye, SA365 Dauphin. Weapons: 4 x 8-cell SYLVER launchers with MBDA Aster 15 surface-to-air missiles; 2 x 6-cell Sadral launchers with Mistral short-range missiles; 8 x Giat 20F2 20mm (0.78in) cannon*

LAUNCHED: *1994*

Extended Flight Deck

Trials indicated that Charles de Gaulle's *flight deck needed to be extended in order to operate the E-2C Hawkeye Airborne Early Warning aircraft, resulting in additional delays before she could enter commission. In her first major refit, beginning in 2007, she received a new command and control system that incorporates satellite communications equipment.*

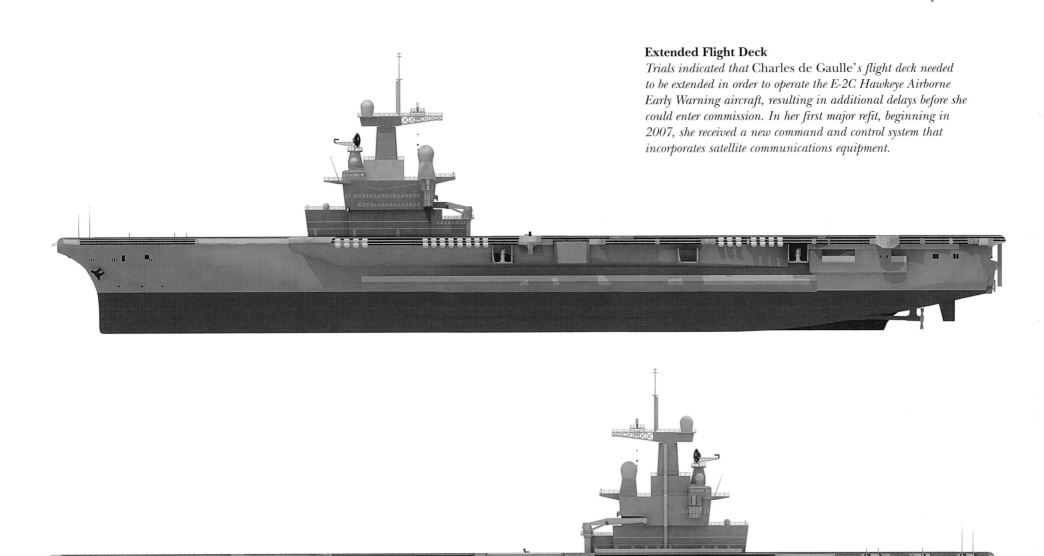

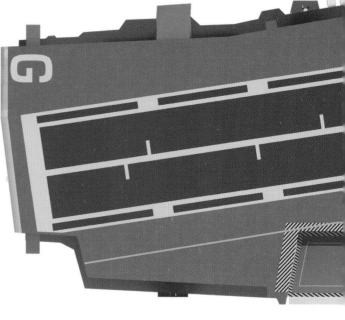

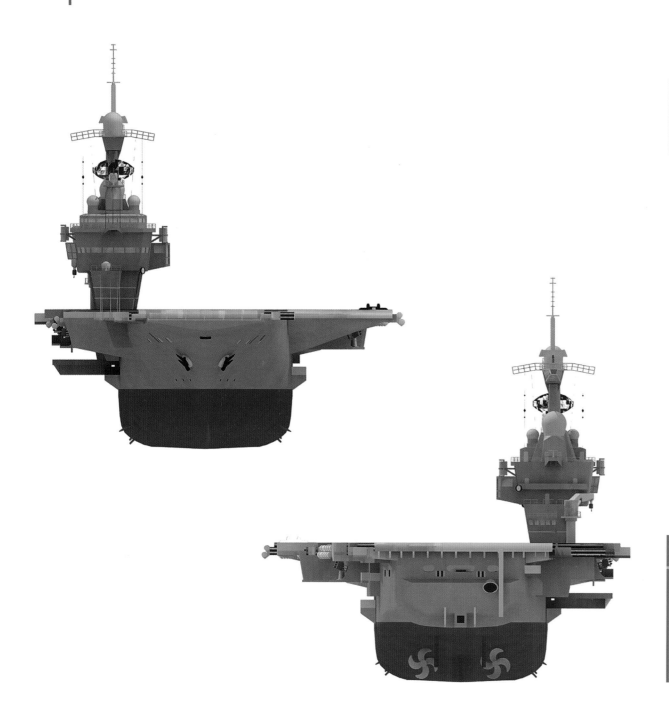

MAIN FEATURES

- Nuclear power gives virtually unlimited operating range
- Air Group of 40 aircraft
- Advanced stabilizing system to minimize pitch, roll and yaw

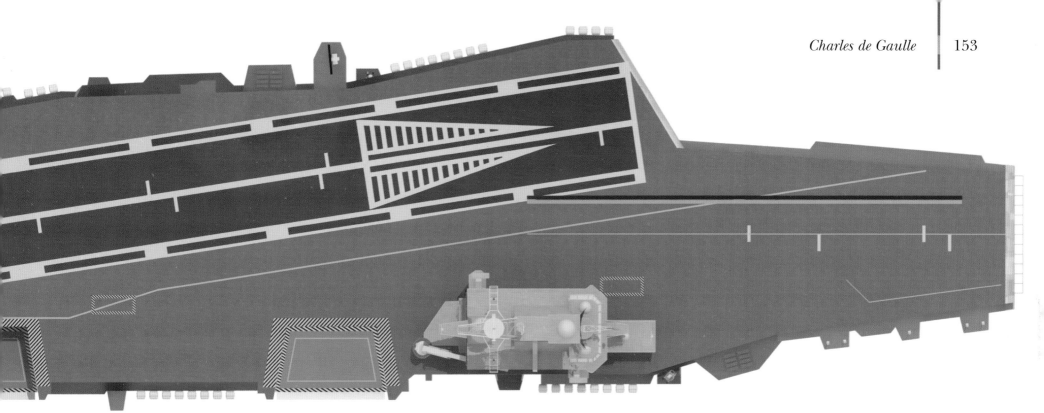

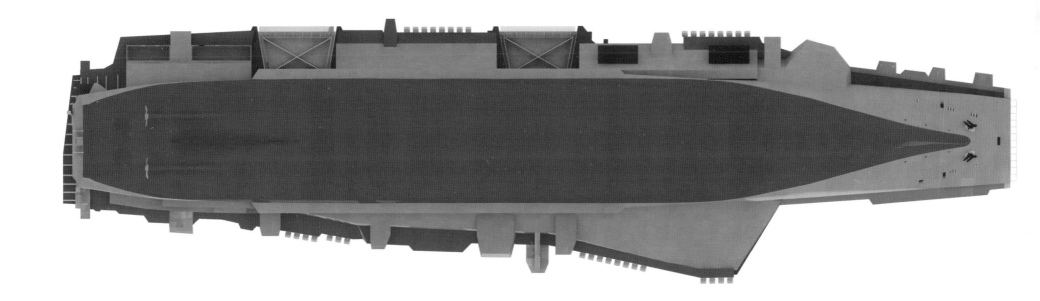

ROLE IN AFGHANISTAN

In 2001, Charles de Gaulle *deployed to the Indian Ocean as part of a French task force operating against the Taliban in Afghanistan. In addition to providing aerial reconnaissance, aircraft from the carrier attacked a number of Taliban targets. Aircraft from* Charles de Gaulle *later engaged in an 'exchange visit' with aircraft from a US carrier, landing on each other's home carrier in a show of solidarity among the allies.* Charles de Gaulle *returned to the Indian Ocean in 2005–2006, again engaging Taliban ground targets in Afghanistan as part of the international Operation Enduring Freedom.*

Winston S. Churchill

USS *Winston S. Churchill* is an Arleigh Burke class destroyer in service with the United States Navy. The Arleigh Burke class was built around the Aegis air defence system first used in the Ticonderoga class cruisers, and also incorporates a number of stealth features. It is unusual for a US warship to be named after a British leader, but USS *Winston S. Churchill* is a symbol of the close alliance between Britain and the United States. A Royal Navy officer serves aboard her, and the White Ensign is flown along with the Stars and Stripes. The Arleigh Burke class carries a powerful armament, including long-range cruise missiles, anti-ship missiles, a 127mm (5in) gun, surface-to-air missiles and anti-submarine torpedoes, with close-in weapon systems for last-ditch missile defence. Some vessels of the class have been fitted with remote mine-hunting equipment, and are being upgraded to handle theatre ballistic missile defence.

SPECIFICATIONS

TYPE: *Destroyer*

COUNTRY OF ORIGIN: *United States of America*

DISPLACEMENT: *9350 tonnes (9202 long tons)*

DIMENSIONS: *Length: 155m (509ft) Beam: 20m (66ft) Draught: 9.4m (31ft)*

MACHINERY: *4 x General Electric LM2500-30 gas turbines; two shafts*

MAXIMUM SPEED: *30 knots (56km/h)*

ARMAMENT: *Aircraft: SH-60 Seahawk LAMPS III helicopters. Weapons: 1 x 32-cell, 1 x 64-cell Mk 41 vertical launch systems; 96 x RIM-66 SM-2 Standard, BGM-109 Tomahawk, or RUM-139 VL-Asroc missiles; 1 x 127mm (5in)/62 cal., 2 x 25mm (0.98in), 2 x .50 cal. guns (single), 2 x .50 cal. (dual), 2 x 7.62mm (0.3in) M240 guns, 2 x 20mm (0.78in) Phalanx CIWS; 2 x Mk 46 triple torpedo tubes*

LAUNCHED: *1999*

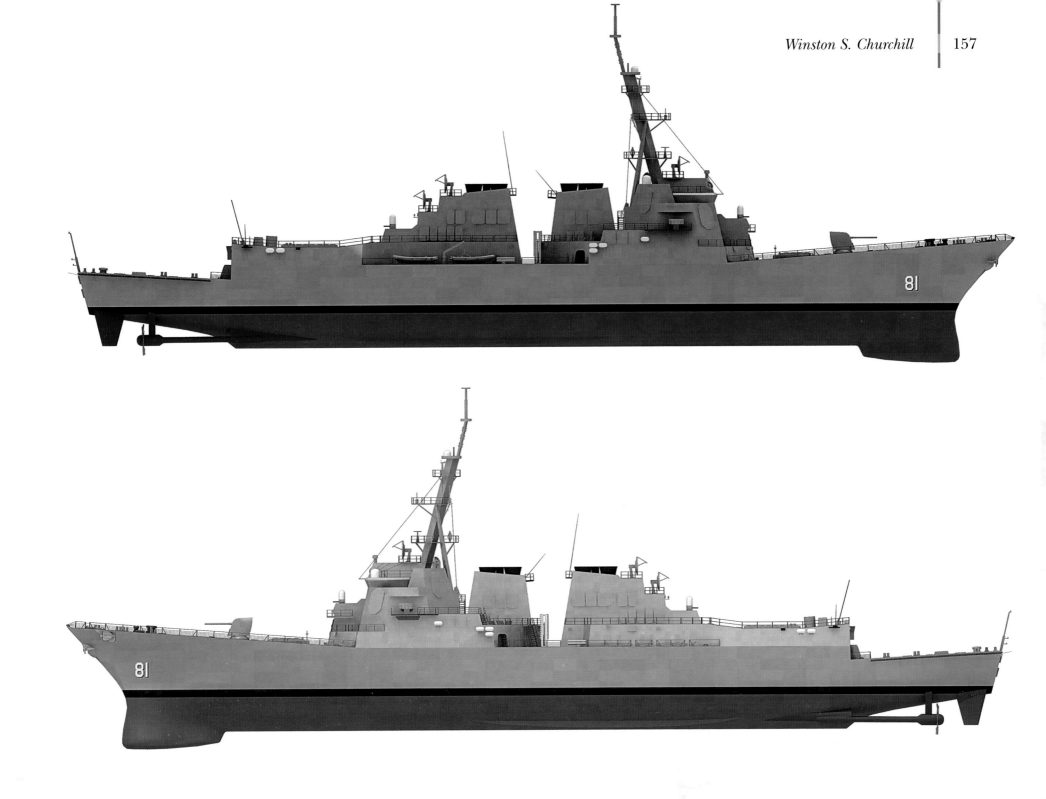

Armour Protection

Modern warships do not carry thick armour like the battleships of previous generations, but there is a gradual move towards increased protection. The Arleigh Burke class dedicates 70 tonnes of her displacement to Kevlar armour, with two additional layers of steel over vital areas. The class was to be replaced by the Zumwalt class, but existing vessels are now being modernized to extend their service lives.

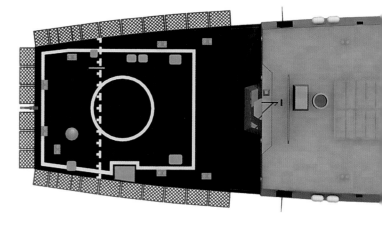

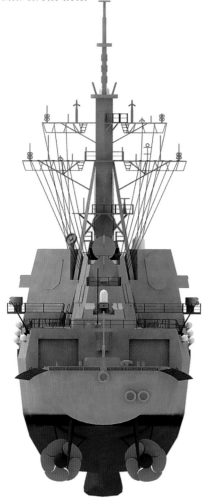

MAIN FEATURES

- Large guided-missile destroyer
- Heavy armament capable of engaging surface, air and submarine targets
- Collective Protection System for defence against nuclear, biological and chemical threats

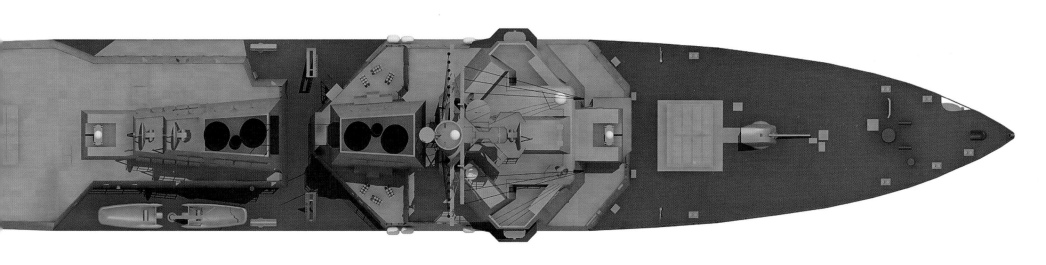

GOODWILL VISITS

USS Winston S. Churchill *was commissioned in 2001, and since then has undertaken a number of goodwill visits, notably to the United Kingdom, as well as deployments to the Persian Gulf. In 2006 she captured a suspected pirate vessel off Somalia, carrying out one of the oldest of naval missions: the protection of commercial traffic.*

Visby

The Visby class corvette is a 'stealth ship' incorporating advanced low-observable technologies. Its hull form and the materials used reduce its radar return, as well as its optical and thermal signature. This not only permits the Visby class to sneak up on a target and attack by surprise, but also increases the vessel's survivability by making it difficult for an opponent to target weapons, even when the corvette has been detected. The Visby class can be fitted out for a range of roles, including mine countermeasures, anti-submarine and surface warfare. Exactly what weapons fit will be carried aboard any given vessel may vary considerably, but all will carry an advanced 57mm (2.24in) gun whose mount is designed for minimal radar return. Anti-ship missiles are likely to also be standard on all vessels, with some carrying mine countermeasures equipment, depth charges and/or anti-submarine torpedoes. Visby class corvettes can accommodate and refuel a helicopter on a landing pad aft, but are too small to carry one aboard.

SPECIFICATIONS

TYPE: *Stealth corvette*

COUNTRY OF ORIGIN: *Sweden*

DISPLACEMENT: *640 tonnes (630 long tons)*

DIMENSIONS: *Length: 72.7m (239ft) Beam: 10.4m (34ft) Draught: 2.4m (8ft)*

MACHINERY: *2 x KaMeWa Waterjets; 4 x Honeywell TF 50 A gas turbines; 2 x MTU Friedrichshafen 16V 2000 N90 diesel engines*

MAXIMUM SPEED: *35 knots (65km/h)*

ARMAMENT: *1 x Bofors 57 Mk 3 gun; 8 x RBS15 Mk2 AshM; mines and depth charges*

LAUNCHED: *2000*

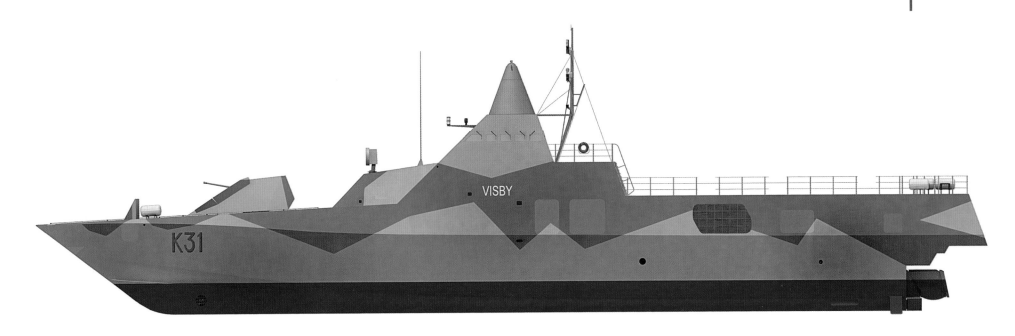

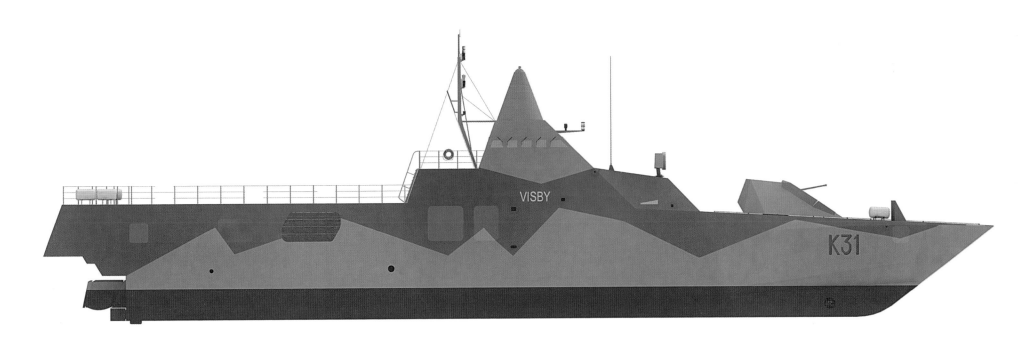

Maximizing Stealth

The Visby class is constructed with an absolute minimum of clutter above decks, to ensure that its radar return is as low as possible. Anti-ship missiles are launched vertically through deck hatches and the main gun barrel is concealed inside the turret when not in use. Air and missile defence is placed in the hands of an advanced decoy system in the event that the stealthy corvette does not evade attack entirely.

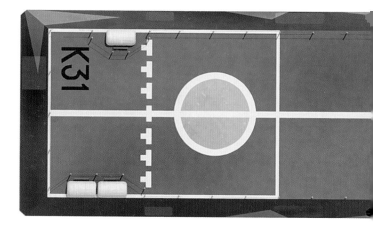

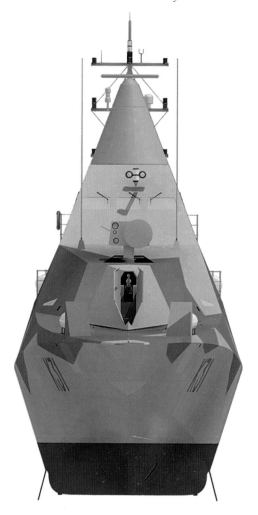

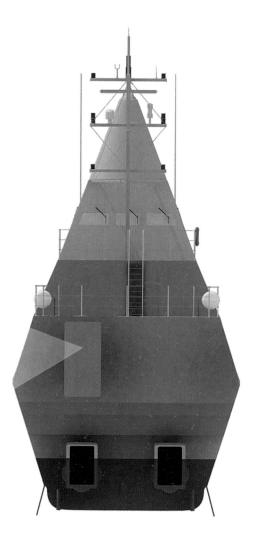

MAIN FEATURES

- Small multirole combatant
- Armament varies by role
- Distinctive 'stealth ship' configuration

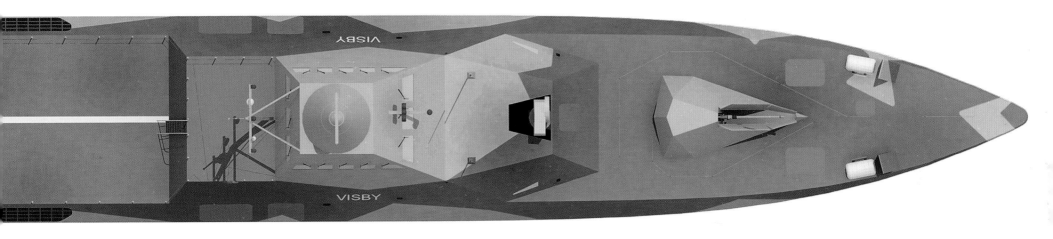

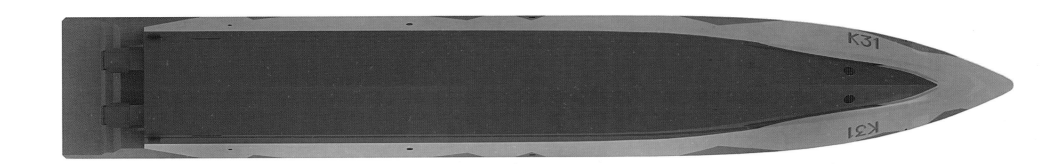

EXPENSIVE AMBITION

As with any ambitious and highly advanced project, the Visby class represented a significant financial risk. Development costs have been high and the project suffered from delays, making each vessel far more expensive than its size would suggest. The stealth capabilities of the Visby class may eventually justify the cost. Only a handful are in service with the Swedish navy, but it is possible that funding may be made available for others at a later date.

Hamburg

F220 *Hamburg* is a modern air-defence frigate of the F124 Sachsen class, currently in service with the German navy. These vessels were designed and built as part of a cooperation agreement between Germany, Spain and the Netherlands. Although classed as frigates, the ships of the Sachsen class are larger than the destroyers that previously fulfilled their role. Anti-aircraft armament includes medium and long-range surface-to-air missiles launched from a vertical launch system, plus a short-range surface-to-air system for point defence. A general-purpose gun armament of one 76mm (3in) and two 20mm (0.78in) guns are shipped, along with Harpoon missiles for anti-surface warfare and homing torpedoes for anti-submarine work.

SPECIFICATIONS

TYPE: *Frigate*

COUNTRY OF ORIGIN: *Germany*

DISPLACEMENT: *5690 tonnes (5600 long tons)*

DIMENSIONS: *Length: 143m (469ft) Beam: 17m (56ft) Draught: 5m (16ft)*

MACHINERY: *2 x MTU V20 diesel engines; 1 x General Electric LM2500 gas turbine; 2 propeller shafts*

MAXIMUM SPEED: *29 knots (54km/h)*

ARMAMENT: *Aircraft: 2 x Sea Lynx Mk.88A or NH90 helicopters. Weapons: 1 x MK. 41 VLS Tactical with 8 cells for 32 RIM-162 ESSM (4 per cell) and 24 SM-2 IIIA surface-to-air missiles; 2 x RAM launchers with 21 surface-to-air/CIWS-missiles each; 2 x quadruple Harpoon anti-ship missile launchers; 1 x OTO-Melara 76mm (3in) dual-purpose gun; 2 x Mauser MLG 27 27mm (1.06in) autocannons; 2 x triple torpedo launchers with EuroTorp MU90 Impact torpedoes*

LAUNCHED: *2001*

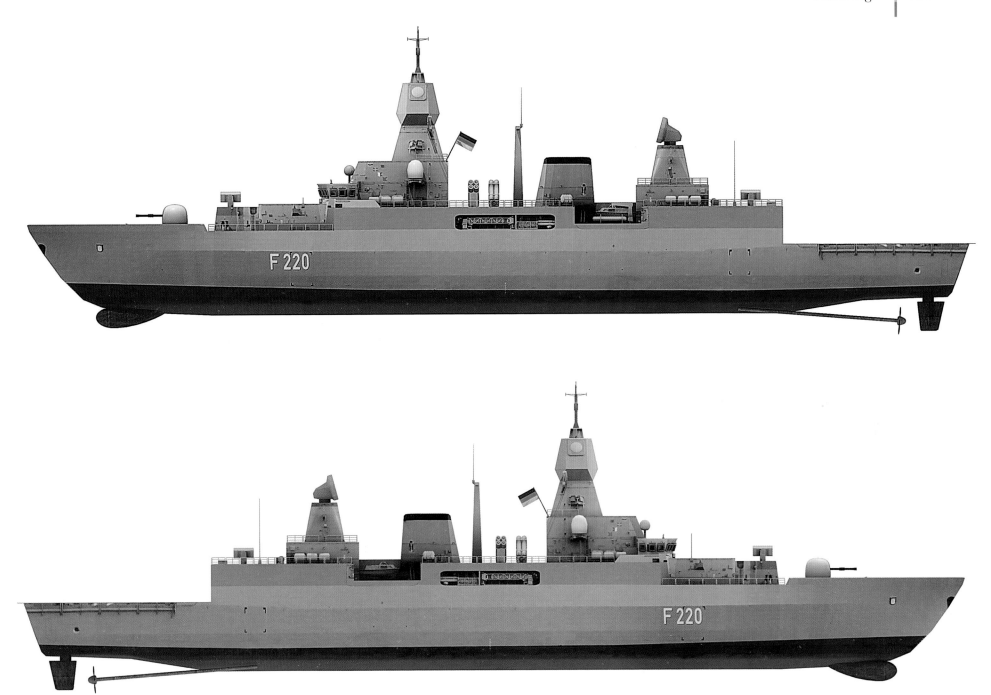

Computer-controlled Helicopter System

Hamburg's flight deck uses a computer-controlled helicopter handling system to assist landings and secure a helicopter once it is down. She was also fitted with a 155mm (6.1in) gun turret capable of attacking targets more than 20 nautical miles inshore. The weapon system was successfully demonstrated, but the other vessels have not been refitted to carry it.

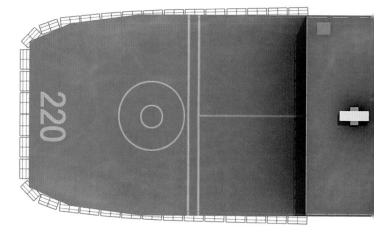

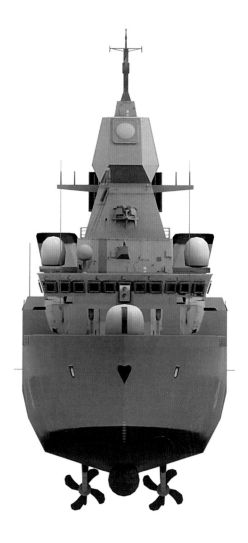

MAIN FEATURES

- Multirole frigate capable of dealing with a wide range of threats
- Main armament of vertically launched missiles
- Extensive electronic countermeasures (ECM) suite and decoy system for missile defence

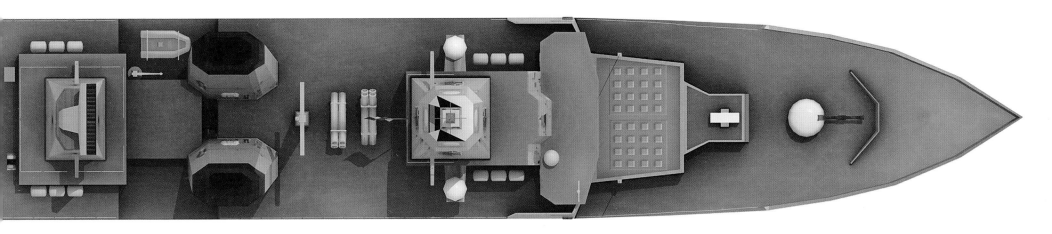

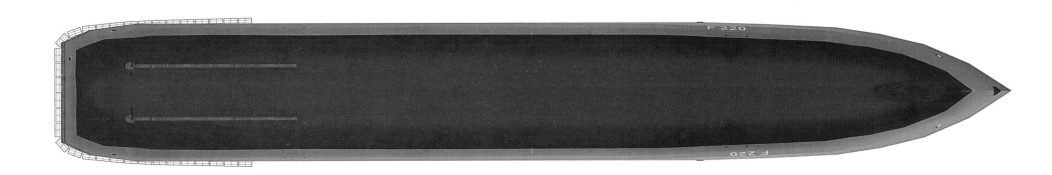

ANTI-AIR PLATFORM

F219 Sachsen *is the name ship of the class. Like her two sisters, she is assigned to 2nd Frigate Squadron based at Wilhelmshaven. In service since 2003, each member of the Sachsen class has room for two helicopters. They are primarily anti-air platforms, but Sachsen-class frigates can carry out a range of missions and deal with threats above, below or on the surface. Although they are expensive, these vessels broad capabilities may well justify their cost.*

F 219

Ronald Reagan

USS *Ronald Reagan* is a Nimitz-class nuclear-powered aircraft carrier in service with the US Navy. Members of the Nimitz class are the largest warships ever built, yet are capable of sustained speeds of more than 30 knots. Range is effectively unlimited due to nuclear power, although air operations are limited by the ability to resupply with aviation fuel and munitions. USS *Reagan* is armed with surface-to-air missiles and a missile-based close-in weapon system for point-defence against missile attack. Its main capabilities, however, rest with the air group. This consists of more than 80 aircraft, including F/A-18 Hornets, which can handle both air-to-air and strike missions. These are backed up by airborne early warning, electronic warfare and anti-submarine warfare (ASW) aircraft, plus helicopters for ASW and utility tasks including rescue of downed pilots. USS *Ronald Reagan* is the only US aircraft carrier to be named in honour of a former US president who was at the time still alive. She is home-ported in San Diego, California.

SPECIFICATIONS

TYPE: *Aircraft carrier*

COUNTRY OF ORIGIN: *United States of America*

DISPLACEMENT: *103,027 tonnes (101,400 long tons)*

DIMENSIONS: *Length: 332m (1089ft) Beam: 76.8m (252ft) Draught: 11.3m (37ft)*

MACHINERY: *2 x Westinghouse A4W nuclear reactors; 4 x steam turbines; 4 x shafts*

MAXIMUM SPEED: *30 knots (56km/h)*

ARMAMENT: *Aircraft: 90 fixed wing aircraft and helicopters. Weapons: 2 x Mk 29 Sea Sparrow; 2 x RIM-116 Rolling Airframe Missile*

LAUNCHED: *2001*

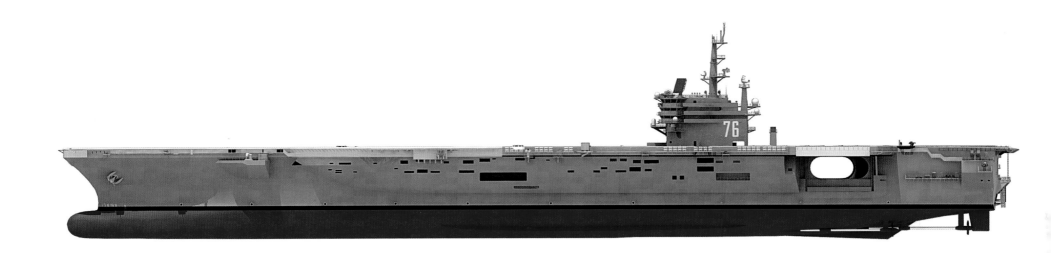

Angled Landing Deck

All large modern aircraft carriers use an angled landing deck and a forward takeoff deck to enable launch and recovery operations to be conducted simultaneously. The angled deck is also safer because it means that landing aircraft are not headed straight down the main deck towards any parked aircraft or personnel working there.

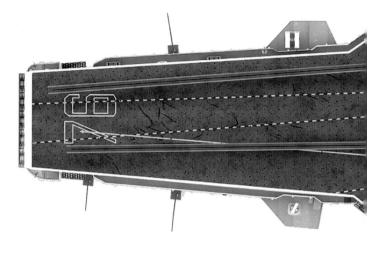

MAIN FEATURES

- Huge nuclear-powered supercarrier
- Large air group capable of undertaking a range of tasks
- Advanced integrated sensor and electronics system

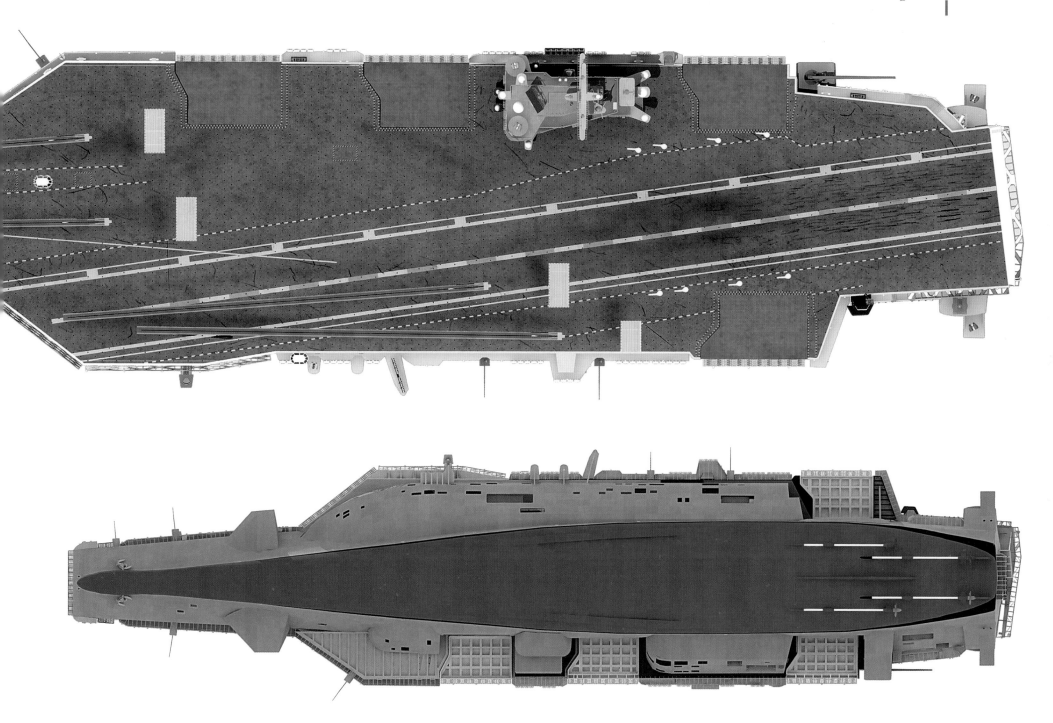

MODERN FLEXIBILITY

Commissioned in 2003, USS Ronald Reagan's *first combat deployment was to the Persian Gulf in 2006, where her air group assisted operations in both Iraq and Afghanistan, as well as increasing the security of nearby seaways. She has also made the most expensive medical house call in history, going to the assistance of a passenger aboard a cruise ship who needed an emergency appendectomy. In 2008, USS* Reagan *demonstrated the flexibility of modern naval forces when she took part in humanitarian relief operations in the Philippines, before deploying off the coast of Afghanistan to assist ground forces fighting insurgents there.*

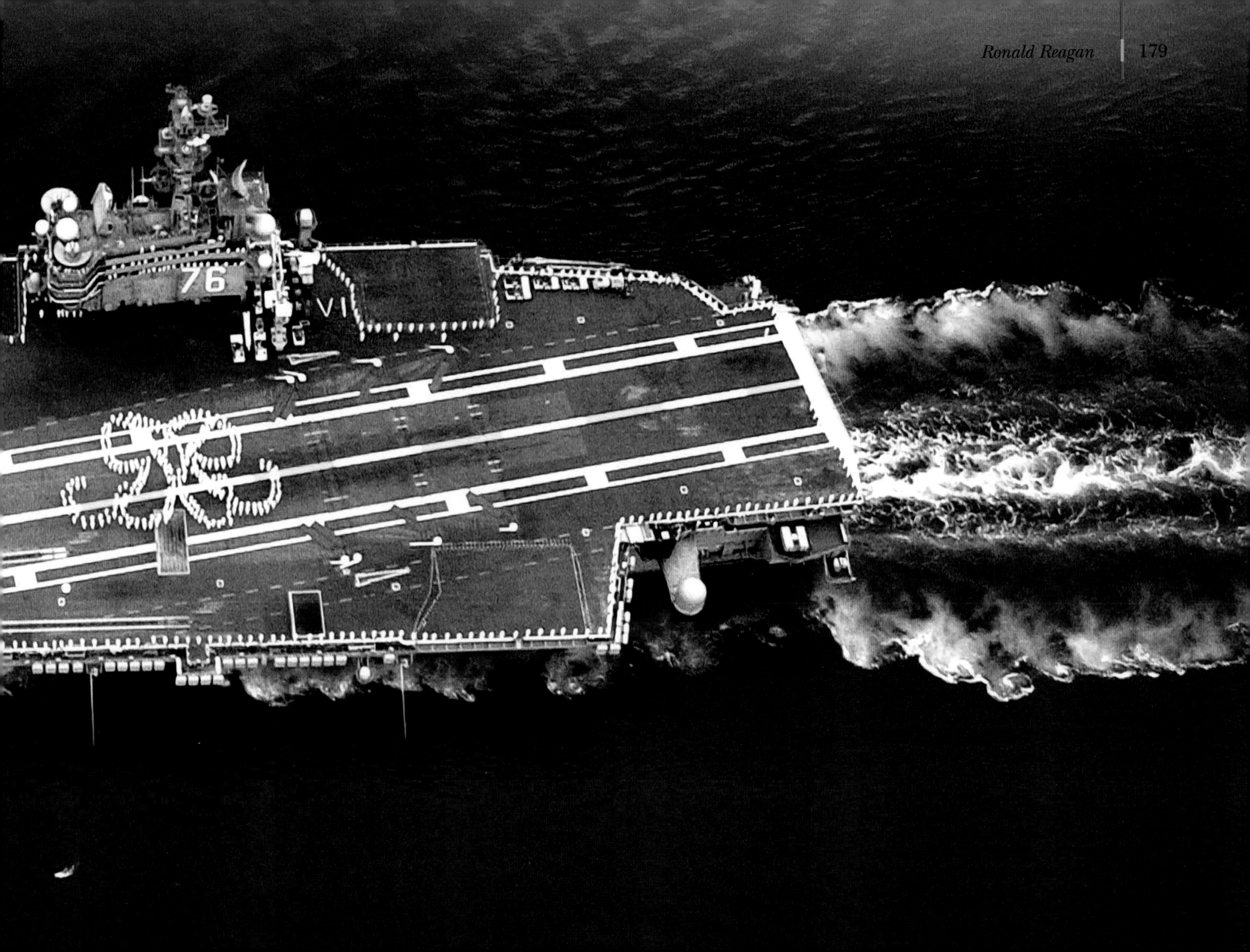
76
VI

Type 022 (Houbei Class)

The Type 022, or Houbei class, of missile boats entered service with the People's Liberation Army Navy of China in 2004. A departure from the previous Chinese practice of building very conventional boats based on Russian designs, the Type 022 is built on a wave-piercing catamaran hull form and uses waterjet propulsion to give a top speed of up to 38 knots. It is armed with launchers for eight anti-ship or land-attack missiles. A light surface-to-air missile launcher provides air defence, with a six-barrel 30mm (1.18in) cannon as a backup. This weapon also enables the class to undertake general patrol duties where a heaver gun, or missiles, would not be appropriate. The comprehensive electronics fit and high degree of automation make these vessels a significant investment, rather than a cheap coastal defence force.

SPECIFICATIONS

TYPE: *Missile boat*

COUNTRY OF ORIGIN: *China*

DISPLACEMENT: *224 tonnes (220 long tons)*

DIMENSIONS: *Length: 42.6m (140ft) Beam: 12.2m (40ft) Draught: 1.5m (5ft)*

MACHINERY: *2 x diesel engines with 4 MARI waterjet propulsors*

MAXIMUM SPEED: *38 knots (70km/h)*

ARMAMENT: *8 x C-801/802/803 anti-ship missiles or 8 Hongniao land attack missiles; 1 x FLS-1 surface-to-air launcher with 12 x QW class MANPAD missiles; 1 x licensed KBP AO-18 6-barrel 30mm (1.18in) gun*

LAUNCHED: *2004*

Advanced Hull Design

The Small Waterplane Area Twin Hull (SWATH) design used by the Type 022 minimizes drag as with other catamaran types, but is more stable in rough seas. It requires an advanced control system and is significantly more expensive than more conventional hull designs. These are sophisticated vessels all round. The cannon can function as a close-in weapon system to defeat incoming missiles, an expensive feature not usually found on small craft.

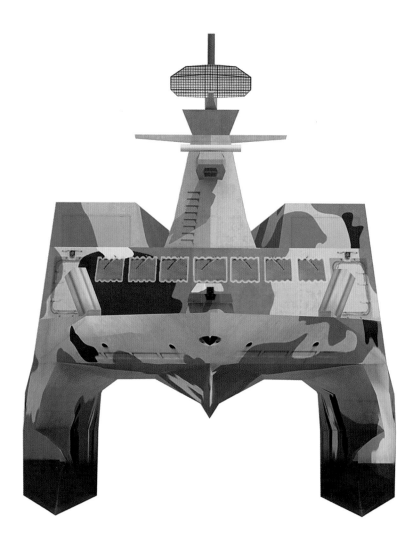

MAIN FEATURES

- Fast attack craft using advanced technology
- Main armament of anti-ship missiles
- Catamaran hull form

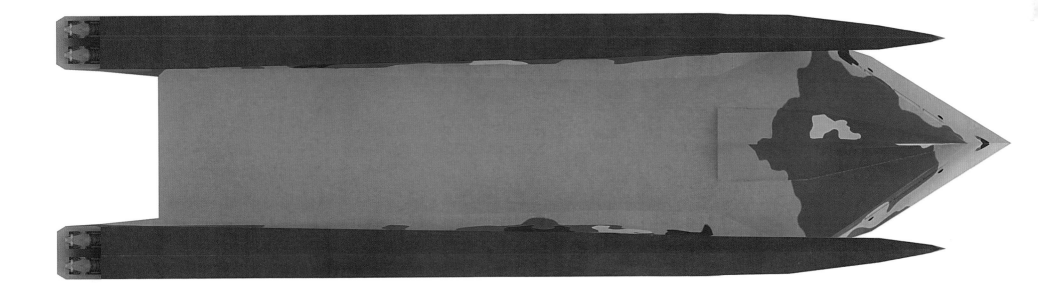

MARINE CAMOUFLAGE

The Type 022 is being built in large numbers. Type 022 vessels are given different camouflage schemes depending on their area of operations. Those based in southerly regions use a somewhat brighter camouflage scheme, with less black and grey than this northern-based boat.

Mistral

The French Mistral class consists of helicopter-carrying vessels designed primarily for the amphibious assault role, but capable of carrying out a range of other tasks. Capable of operating 16–35 helicopters, depending on the type, vessels of this sort can launch 'over-the-beach' strikes, sending a force of marines inland without having to land on a potentially hostile coastline from boats. Not intended to fight other ships, the Mistral class is very lightly armed for air defence. It can carry tanks and up to 900 troops, or other cargo. These vessels have advanced communications equipment, enabling them to function as command posts. It is possible to provide command facilities for a multi-service and/or multinational force. This type of ship can also be employed for disaster relief, using helicopters to reach remote areas with supplies and relief workers, plus military personnel to protect them. A 69-bed hospital with two operating theatres is carried, with the capability to set up a field hospital in the helicopter hangar as needed.

SPECIFICATIONS

Type: *Amphibious assault ship*

Country of Origin: *France*

Displacement: *21,300 tonnes (20,964 long tons)*

Dimensions: *Length: 199m (653ft) Beam: 32m (105ft) Draught: 6.3m (21ft)*

Machinery: *2 x Mermaïd electric motors*

Maximum Speed: *18.8 knots (35km/h)*

Armament: *Aircraft: 16 heavy or 35 light helicopters. Weapons: 2 x Simbad systems; 2 x 30mm (1.18in) Breda-Mauser; 4 x 12.7mm (.5in) M2-HB Browning machine guns*

Launched: *2004*

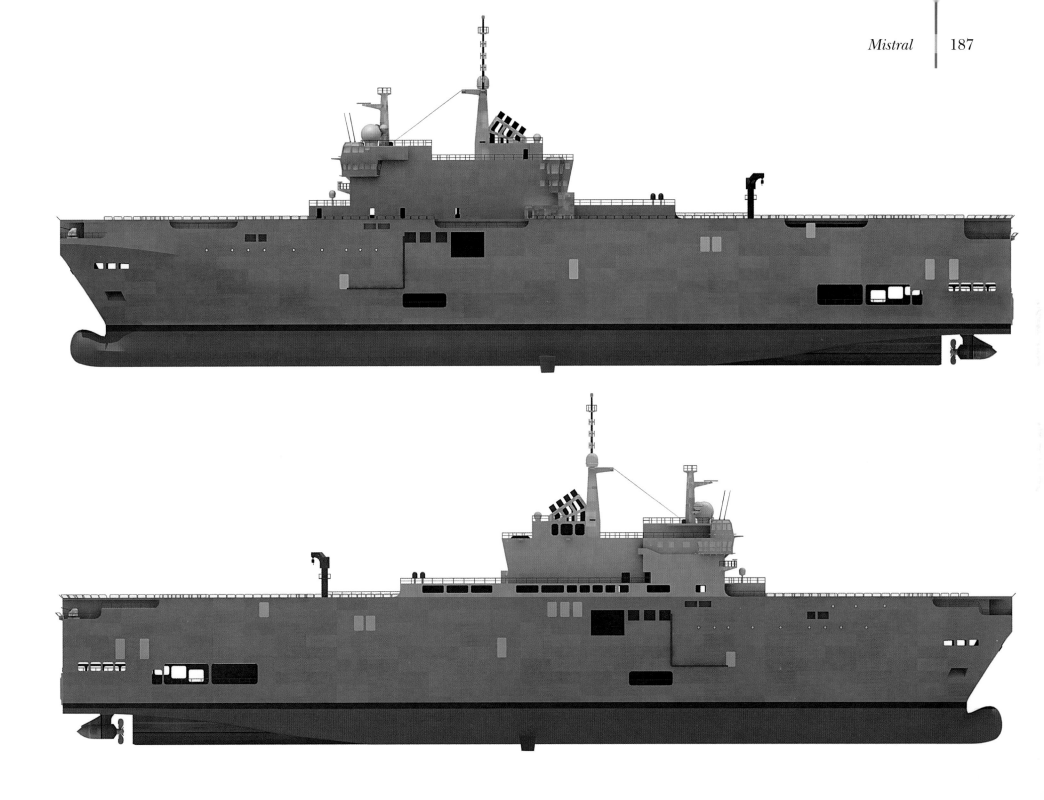

All-Electric Propulsion

The Mistral class is the first French warship to use all-electric propulsion. Two 7MW motors each drive a five-bladed propeller. Power is generated using a diesel system.

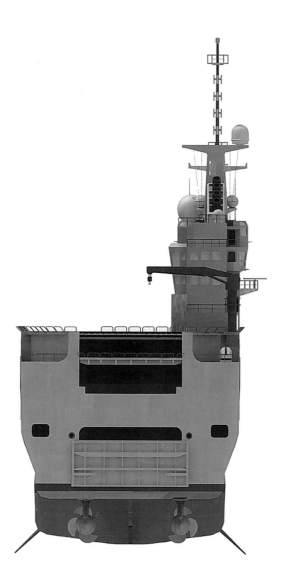

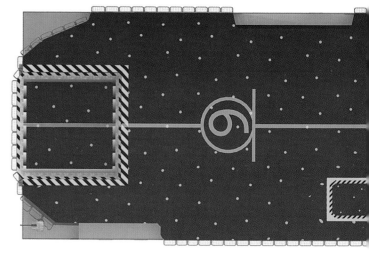

MAIN FEATURES

- Helicopter carrier with command and amphibious assault capabilities
- Light air defence armament
- Can carry one-third of a mechanized regiment

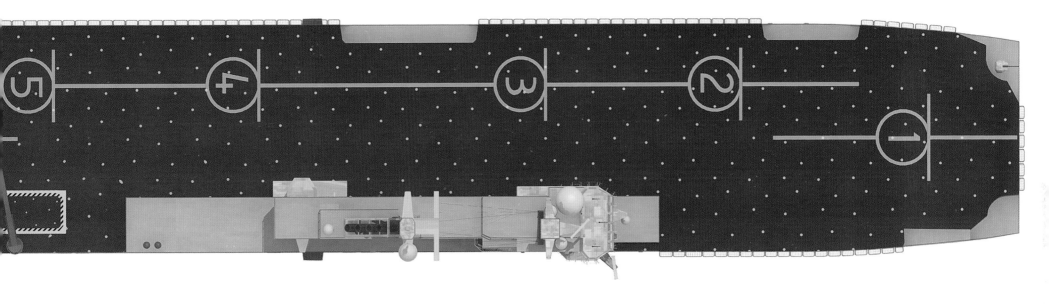

CHANGING ROLE

The Mistral class entered service in 2005, and represents the changing role of naval forces. Not only is this class built with warfighting in mind, with the ability to land tanks, artillery and troops on a hostile shore, but it is equally capable of responding to a humanitarian crisis anywhere in the world. It has thus far been a success, both operationally and on the export market. Two Mistral-class vessels are currently in service with the French navy: the Mistral *and the* Tonnerre. *Work on a third vessel,* Dixmude, *began in 2009. The Russian navy has also ordered one vessel, with the option to buy more.*

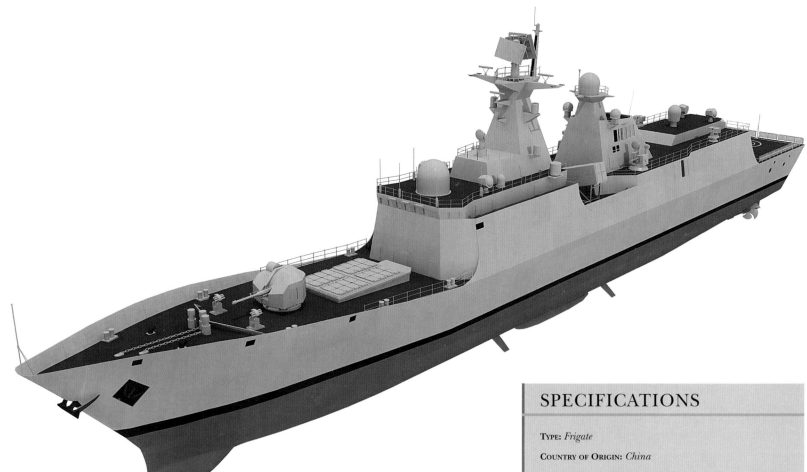

Type 054A Frigate

The Type 054A Frigate (also known as *Jiangkai-II*), a multirole missile frigate incorporating several low-observable ('stealth') features, is operated by the People's Liberation Army Navy of China. It was developed from the preceding Type 054 class, but has updated sensors and is much more capable, especially in terms of air defence. Indeed, this is thought to be the main role envisaged for the class. The Type 054A is capable of engaging surface, submarine and aircraft targets, and can also launch land-attack missiles. Most of the missile armament is carried in a 32-cell vertical launch system, which may be able to launch torpedo delivery missiles.

SPECIFICATIONS

Type: *Frigate*

Country of Origin: *China*

Displacement: *4000 tonnes (3937 long tons)*

Dimensions: *Length: 134m (440ft) Beam: 16m (52ft)*

Machinery: *4 x SEMT Pielstick 16 PA6 STC diesels*

Maximum Speed: *30 knots (56km/h)*

Armament: *Aircraft: 1 x Kamov Ka-28 'Helix' or Harbin Z-9C helicopter. Weapons: 1 x HQ-16 32-cell VLS SAM launcher; 2 x 4 C-803 anti-ship/land-attack cruise missiles; 1 x 76mm (3in) dual purpose gun; 2 x Type 730 7-barrel 30mm (1.18in) CIWS guns; Triple 324mm (12.75in) YU-7 ASW torpedoes; 2 x Type 726-4 18-tube decoy rocket launchers*

Launched: *2006*

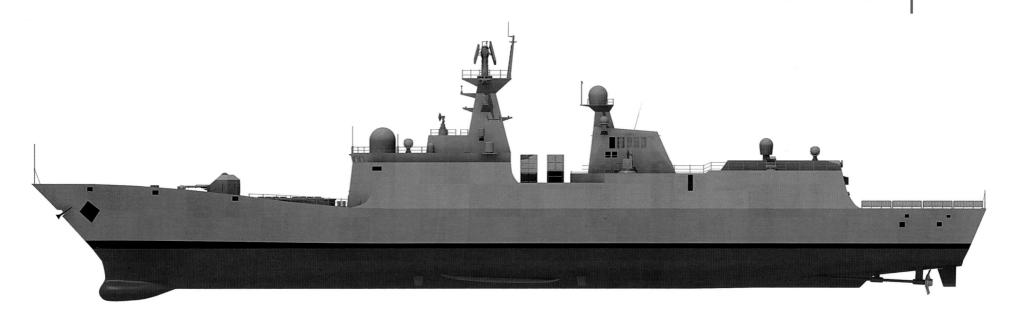

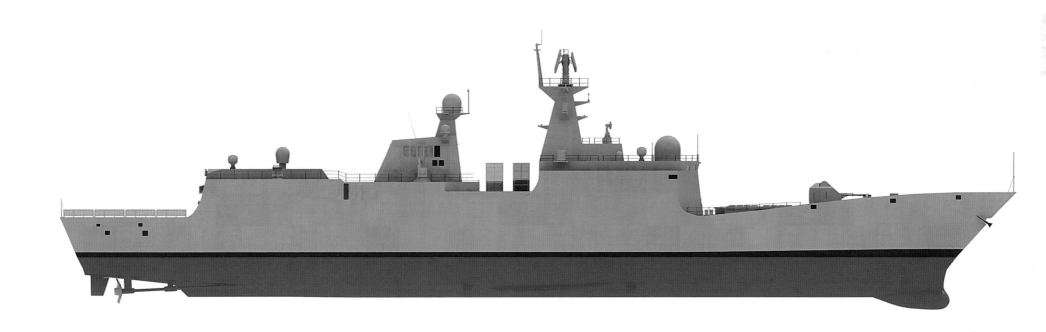

Anti-Shipping and Land-Attack Missiles
The anti-ship/land-attack missiles are carried in two quadruple launchers amidships and can attack targets up to 180 km (110 miles) distant. Anti-submarine torpedoes are carried, along with a 76mm (3in) gun. Two 30mm (1.18in) close-in weapon systems are also fitted, replacing the four mounted on the preceding Type 054 vessels. There are two 18-barrel launchers located amidships, which are thought to be thermal/radar decoy systems.

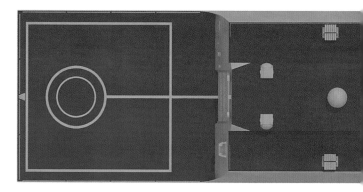

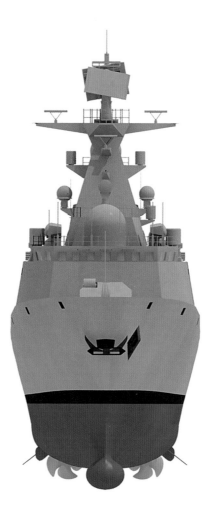

MAIN FEATURES

- Multirole guided missile frigate
- Armed with vertical-launch missiles
- Improved version of Type 054 class

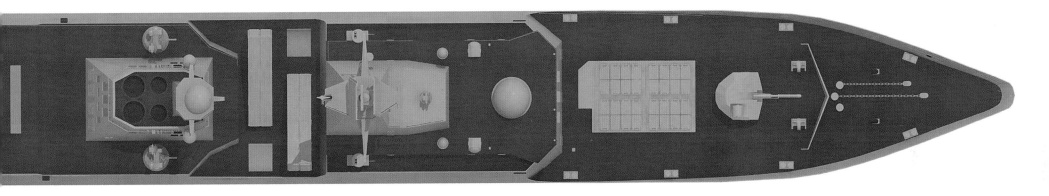

POWER PROJECTION

The Type 054A is characteristic of the development of the Chinese navy. Increasingly, China is becoming capable of projecting naval power into distant waters, even in areas where the air threat is high. Improved radar and sonar systems, coupled with better processing electronics, have enhanced the offensive and defensive capabilities of the Type 054A class considerably, while the adoption of a more stealthy configuration improves survivability.

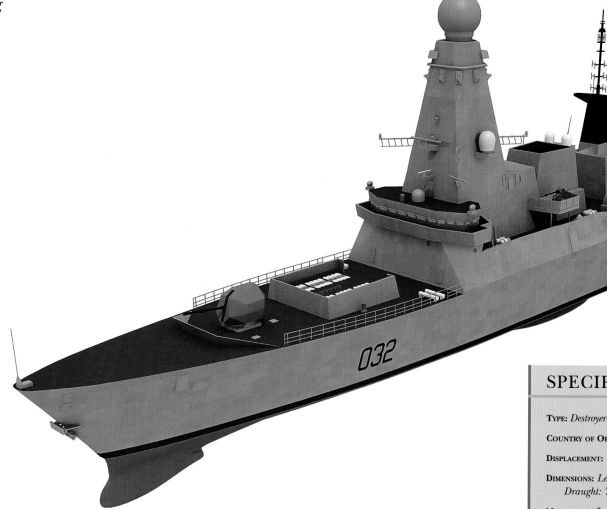

Daring

The British Type 45 Destroyer – also known as the D, or Daring, class – was designed specifically to replace an earlier class, the Type 42, in the same role. Its intended task is area air defence for a task force or fleet, although it can undertake a range of tasks, including surface action and gunfire support of forces ashore. HMS *Daring* will be its lead ship. The Daring class carries surface-to-air missiles as its primary armament, using the Principal Anti-Aircraft Missile System (PAAMS), which was initially developed for use aboard a cancelled multinational frigate project. The PAAMS system launches the Aster 15 missile for short-range air and missile defence and the Aster 30 for more distant targets. A 114mm (4.5in) medium-calibre gun and two 30mm (1.18in) cannon are carried as a general-purpose armament. There is provision for two close-in weapon systems, but these are not fitted.

SPECIFICATIONS

TYPE: *Destroyer*

COUNTRY OF ORIGIN: *United Kingdom*

DISPLACEMENT: *7500 tonnes (7382 long tons)*

DIMENSIONS: *Length: 152.4m (500ft) Beam: 21.2m (70ft) Draught: 7.4m (24ft)*

MACHINERY: *2 x Rolls-Royce WR-21 gas turbines; 2 x Wärtsilä V12 VASA32 diesel generators; 2 x Converteam electric motors*

MAXIMUM SPEED: *29 knots (54km/h)*

ARMAMENT: *Aircraft: 1 x Lynx HMA8 or 1 x Westland Merlin HM1. Weapons: 1 x PAAMS Air Defence System; 1 x BAE Systems 114mm (4.5in) Mk 8 Mod. 1 gun; 2 x 30mm (1.18in) guns; 2 x Miniguns and up to 6 x General Purpose Machine Guns. Provision for but not fitted with: 2 x Quad Boeing RGM-84 Harpoon launchers (total of 8 missiles); 2 x Phalanx CIWS; BGM-109 Tomahawk cruise missiles*

LAUNCHED: *2006*

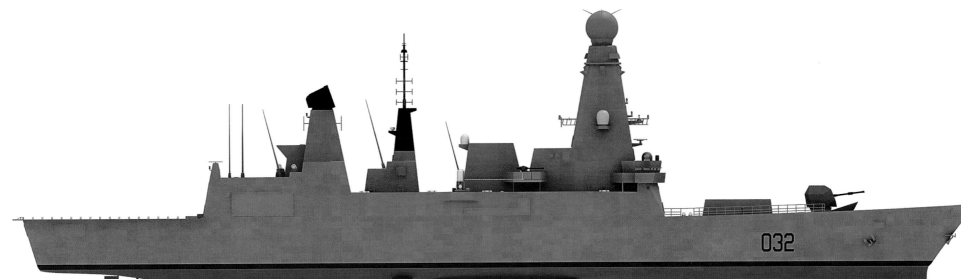

Long-Range Radar System

The most obvious feature of the Type 45 is the large radome located at the top of the mast. This houses a long-range radar system which is essential to vessel's primary function as an air defence platform.
The Type 45 is not a 'stealth ship', but like many modern designs it makes use of low-observable (stealth) technology as part of its defences.

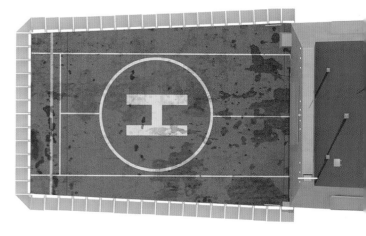

MAIN FEATURES

- Anti-air destroyer
- Integrated missile system for area and point defence against missiles and aircraft
- Torpedo detection system offers advice on evasion and decoy placement

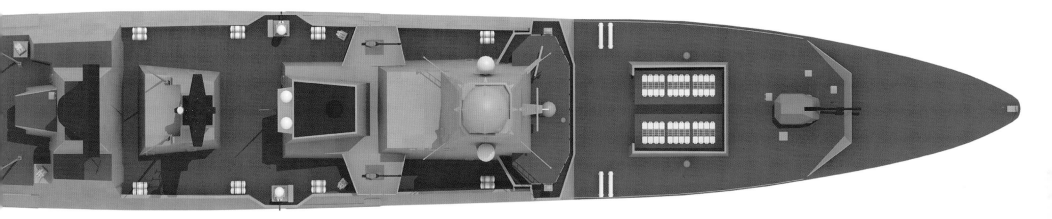

ENDURING DESIGN

The Type 45 class is due in service by 2014 and will serve with the Royal Navy for many years, receiving upgrades and refits to accommodate new technologies. Retrofitting systems can be a problem in 'tight' designs, but the Type 45 was specifically designed with upgrade and modification in mind. Possible modifications include long-range cruise missiles, close-in weapon systems and the addition of a theatre ballistic missile defence capability.

New York

USS *New York* is an amphibious warfare ship designed to transport and support a force of US Marines. The fifth member of the San Antonio class, she is notable for using steel from the wreckage of the World Trade Center in her construction. The San Antonio class is lightly armed for self-protection, with two 30mm (1.18in) close-in weapon systems and surface-to air missiles tied into an integrated ship self-defence system. Its main function is to project power inland, rather than act as a warship in its own right. Troops can be landed by hovercraft, amphibious assault vehicles and Osprey tilt-rotor aircraft. The ability to land troops ashore enables naval forces to project power beyond the coastline; bombardment can only do so much. A landing ship can also be used to quickly get aid into a disaster zone.

SPECIFICATIONS

Type: *Amphibious transport dock*

Country of Origin: *United States of America*

Displacement: *25,300 tonnes (24,900 long tons)*

Dimensions: *208.5m (684ft) Beam: 31.9m (105ft) Draught: 7m (23ft)*

Machinery: *4 x sequentially turbocharged marine Colt-Pielstick diesel engines, two shafts*

Maximum Speed: *22 knots (41km/h)*

Armament: *Aircraft: Launch or land up to 2 x CH-46 Sea Knight or up to two MV-22 Osprey. Weapons: 2 x Bushmaster II 30mm (1.18in) close-in guns; two Rolling Airframe Missile launchers*

Launched: *2007*

'Stealthy' Hull and Superstructure

The USS New York has a number of 'stealth' features, including a hull and superstructure form designed to reduce radar return. She is also protected against shock, blast and fragmentation effects to enhance survivability, and has an advanced decoy system for missile defence.

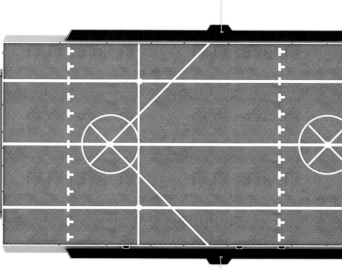

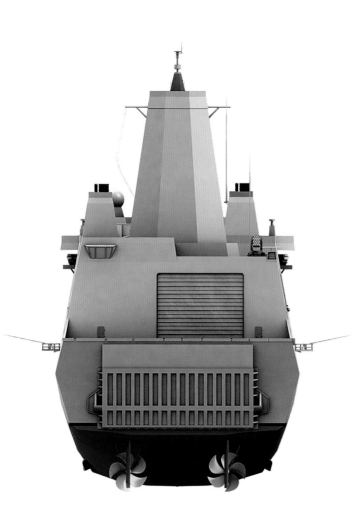

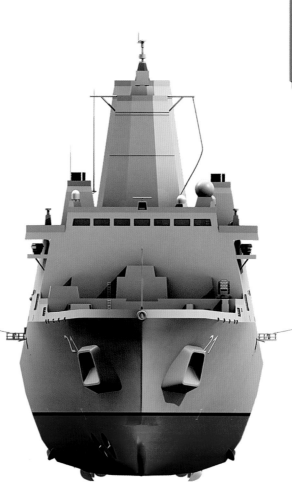

MAIN FEATURES

- Amphibious warfare ship
- Highly integrated defensive armament
- Advanced propeller design reduces drag

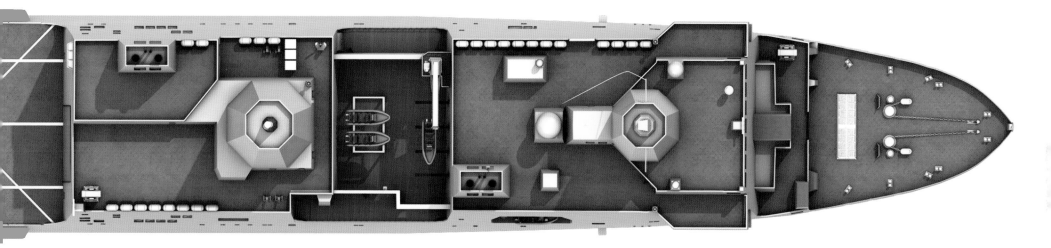

NOTABLE MATERIALS

USS New York*'s structure contains steel from the World Trade Center. Although it comprises a very small fraction of the displacement of the vessel, this steel was treated with almost religious reverence during the ship's construction While landing ships are not the most glamorous of vessels, they are essential to many naval missions.* New York *can carry up to 800 troops, and project power inland using assault craft, hovercraft and aircraft.*

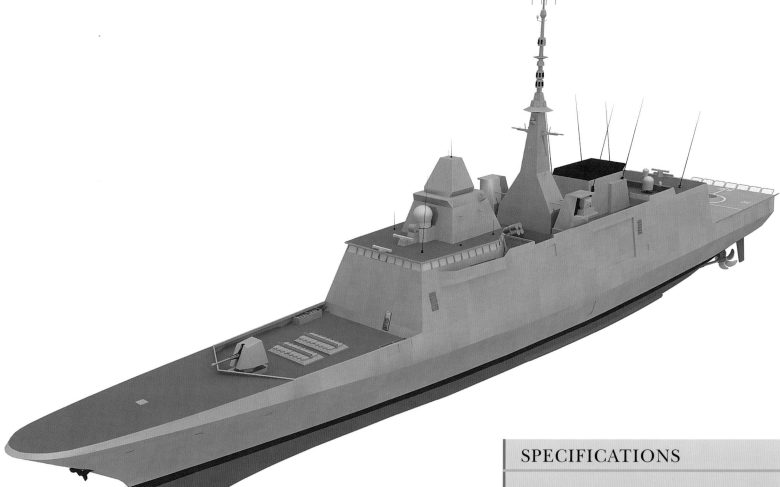

FREMM

The FREMM project is a joint French–Italian venture designed to create a multimission frigate for both navies and foreign markets. The name is derived from the French Fregate Multi-Mission or the Italian Fregata Europea Multi-Missione. Rather than a single class, the FREMM project was designed to create a family of closely related vessels, including an anti-submarine variant, as well as anti-air and multimission versions. All versions of the FREMM frigate carry a 76mm (3in) gun, lighter weapons for air defence and dealing with minor threats, a helicopter and both lightweight anti-submarine torpedoes and anti-ship missiles. With buyers able to tailor FREMM vessels to their unique needs, these ships are a good prospect for international export and have already received orders beyond the navies of the developing partners.

SPECIFICATIONS

Type: *Frigate*

Country of Origin: *France/Italy*

Displacement: *6000 tonnes (5905 long tons)*

Dimensions: *Length: 142m (466ft) Beam: 20m (66ft) Draught: 5m (16ft)*

Machinery: *1 x GE/Avio LM 2500 G4 gas turbine*

Maximum Speed: *27 knots (50km/h)*

Armament: *Aircraft: 1 or 2 helicopters. Weapons: MU 90 torpedoes; MM-40 Exocet or Teseo\Otomat Mk-2/A; MBDA Aster SAAM; Otobreda 76mm (3in) SR gun*

Launched: *2010*

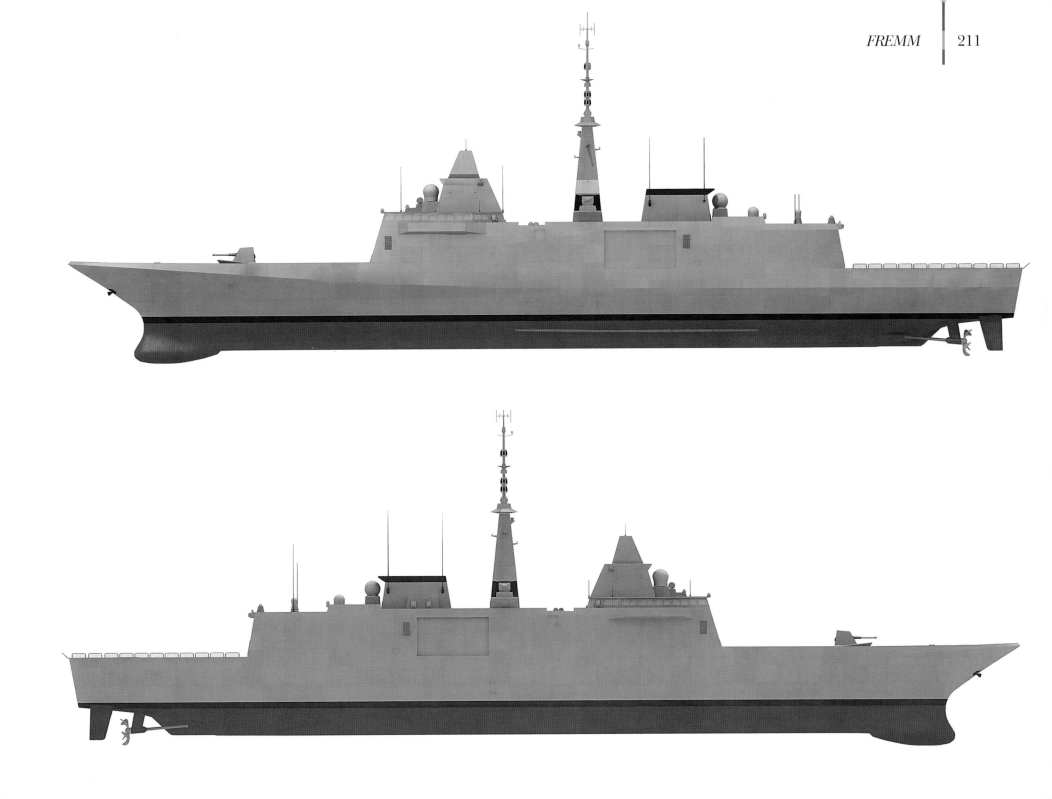

Tailored Flexibility

Additional equipment is tailored to the ship's intended role: anti-submarine variants have a towed array sonar and additional sensors, while the French multirole variant can ship cruise missiles in a vertical launch system. The air-defence version is intended to be capable of carrying either large numbers of anti-air missiles or a mix of missile types, to allow the engagement of land targets as well as aircraft.

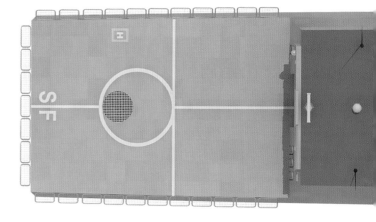

MAIN FEATURES

- Standardized vessel available in three variants for different applications
- General-purpose basic armament can be augmented for any specific role
- Internally spacious design to allow for upgrade and to improve habitability for the crew

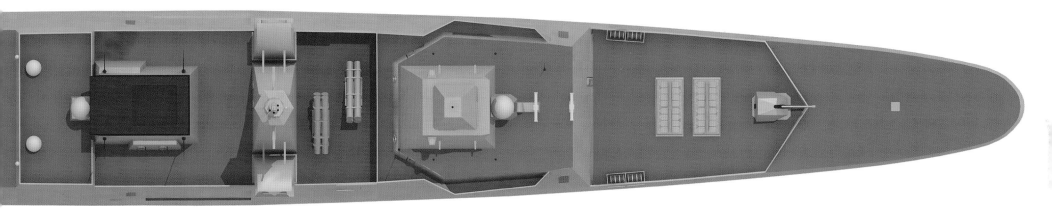

FOREIGN CUSTOM

The distinctive slab sides and clean lines of modern frigates are intended to reduce radar return and thus improve survivability, and the FREMM is no exception. Clutter and sharp angles are kept to a minimum. The class is scheduled for delivery starting in 2011. France intends to operate 11 vessels and Italy six, in both cases replacing older frigates that previously filled the same roles. Although not part of the development project, Morocco and Greece have agreed to buy FREMM vessels, ordering one and six, respectively.

DDX (Zumwalt Class)

The Zumwalt class of advanced multimission destroyers is currently under development for use by the United States Navy. The project has been revised at times to meet changing requirements and to take advantage of new technologies. Rather than being optimized for 'blue water' operations in the open ocean, the Zumwalt class is primarily aimed at the littoral environment close to the shore. The hull uses a 'tumblehome' configuration, sloping inwards rather than outwards above the waterline. Combined with the use of advanced materials, this greatly reduces radar return. Thermal and acoustic emissions are also kept to a minimum, and advanced low-probability-of-intercept radars are utilized, improving 'stealth' characteristics even when actively emitting radar pulses.

SPECIFICATIONS

TYPE: *Destroyer*

COUNTRY OF ORIGIN: *United States of America*

DISPLACEMENT: *14798 tonnes (14564 long tons)*

DIMENSIONS: *Length: 183m (600ft) Beam: 25.6m (84ft) Draught: 8.4m (28ft)*

MACHINERY: *2 x Rolls-Royce Marine Trent-30 gas turbines and emergency diesel generators*

MAXIMUM SPEED: *30.3 knots (56km/h)*

ARMAMENT: *Aircraft: 1 x SH-60 or MH-60R helicopter, 3 x MQ-8 Fire Scout VTUAVs. Weapons: 20 x MK 57 VLS modules; Evolved Sea Sparrow Missile (ESSM); Tactical Tomahawk Vertical Launch Anti-Submarine Rocket (ASROC); 2 x 155mm (6.1in) Advanced Gun System; 2 x Mk 110 57mm (2.24in) gun (CIWS)*

LAUNCHED: *n/a; expected commissioning 2015*

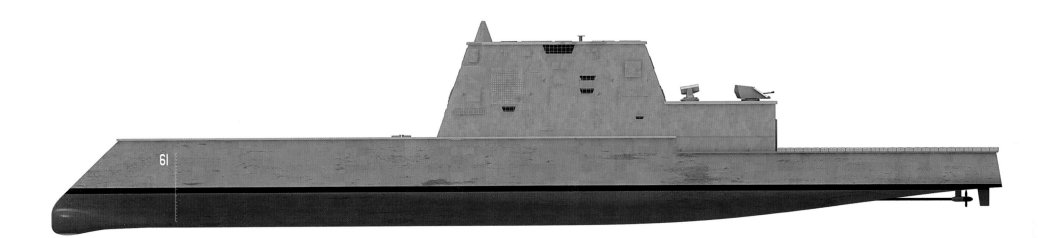

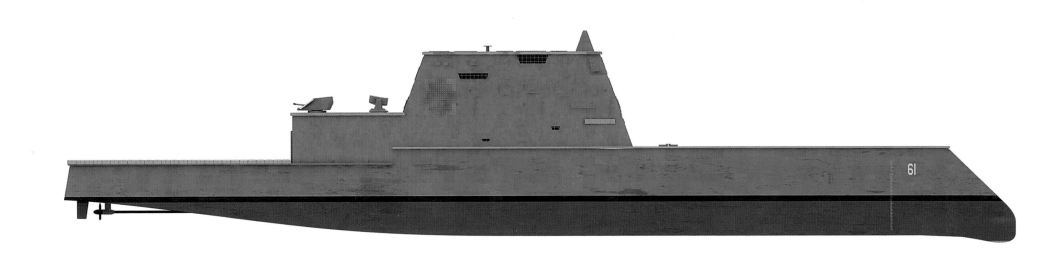

Land and Surface Attack

The Zumwalt class will be armed with two 155mm (6.1in) guns capable of firing 12 rounds per minute at targets up to 100 nautical miles distant, for land attack and engagement of surface combatants. Missile armament will most likely include Tactical Tomahawk cruise missiles in vertical launch tubes dispersed around the hull. Doing this, rather than concentrating them in one area, reduces the effects of damage on the ship's ability to fight and the possibility of a single hit crippling the vessel's armament.

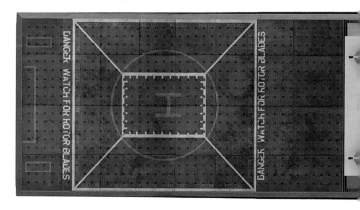

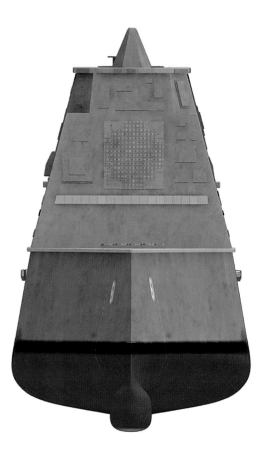

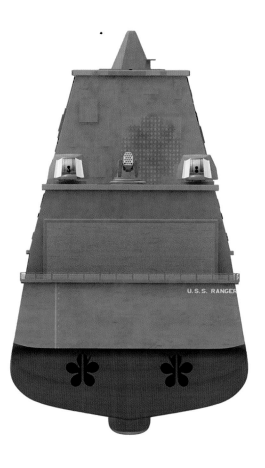

MAIN FEATURES

- Stealthy design optimized for 'brown water' (littoral) operations
- Capable of attacking targets far inland with guns or missiles
- Advanced electric propulsion system

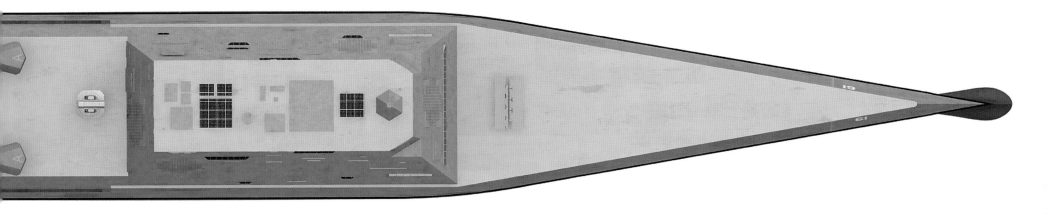

PLANNED SERVICE

In-service date for the Zumwalt class is projected for 2015, although a planned build of 32 vessels has been pared down by budget cuts. It is currently probable that only three vessels will be built. Instead, the US Navy plans to build more of the less expensive Arleigh Burke class, which follows a much more traditional design.

Index

Page references in *italics* refer to illustration captions